TRIDENT TANKERS Ltd.

a change of course

Michael Langley

With best wishes from Mike

MP Middleton Press

cover pic details:
    Top left - see caption 3.
    Middle left - see caption 52.
    Top right - see caption 69
    Bottom - see caption 88.

Notes about the author -

An interest in coastal ships and local harbours grew during school years at Horsham, West Sussex, somewhat amplified by regular cross-Solent trips to the other Family 'stronghold', the Isle of Wight. Later, whilst at Warsash, School of Navigation, an interview with Trident Tankers in London proved positive, and Navigating Cadet's indentures were duly signed at the end of 1965. Some thirteen years later with the Masters Certificate obtained, shore based office employment beckoned, and by this time Trident Tankers Ltd had become P&O Bulk Shipping Division. Following a very brief period in 'Personnel', the next thirteen years passed rapidly working mostly as a Marine Superintendent, in the Technical Department. The Company itself evolved during this period from Bulk Shipping Division to Deep Sea Cargo Division, to P&O Ship Management Ltd. In 1991 redundancy occurred, and later the early interest in coastal shipping revived leading to publication of 'SUSSEX SHIPPING- Sail, Steam & Motor', 'SOLENT- Creeks, Craft & Cargoes', 'KENT SEAWAYS- Hoys to Hovercraft' and lastly, 'SOUTH WEST HARBOURS- Ships & Trades'.

Published February 2009

ISBN 978 1 906008 43 7

© Middleton Press, 2009

Design Deborah Esher

Published by
    Middleton Press
    Easebourne Lane
    Midhurst
    West Sussex
    GU29 9AZ
Tel: 01730 813169
Fax: 01730 812601
Email: info@middletonpress.co.uk
www.middletonpress.co.uk

Printed & bound by MPG Biddles Ltd, Kings Lynn

CONTENTS

PREFACE

What follows might be described as something of a 'hybrid' work as it is essentially a blend of ship type evolution and specific Company history. The mix contains some onboard technical description and detail, plus personal observation peppered with just a hint of nostalgia for an era not so long departed. The story begins with the P&O Group Board's 1955 decision to 'enter the tanker market'. The growing fleet would later diversify into Ore/Bulk/Ore (OBO) carriers, Liquefied Petroleum Gas (LPG) tankers, and become a major player in the dry bulk cargo trades. Many would be the fleet and office reorganisations along the way as world trade patterns, economic factors, and ship technology shifted continuously. For one short operational period the Group's remaining traditional cargo and refrigerated cargo ships (reefers), were united with the oil tankers, gas ships and bulkers as a single entity, yet the final core business settled on the worldwide operation of a fleet of very large dry bulk carriers.

GLOSSARY and ABBREVIATIONS

MV   Motor Vessel
SS   Steam Ship
Tonnages:
Gross Registered Tonnage, abbr. grt. volumetric measure of all enclosed space and
is applied to all ships. 1grt = 100cu.ft. This is a true indicator of a ship's overall size.
Deadweight Tonnage, abbr. dwt. actual weight carrying capacity of the ship in tons, includes fuel, water, stores
etc. plus cargo.
Cubic Metres, abbr. m³. applied most often to describe gas tanker cargo capacity.
Length overall: loa. Measurement to the fore and aft extremities.
Beam or breadth: br. Measurement to maximum width.
Draught: dr. Depth of water required for flotation. Summer laden draught normally given.
Engine and Machinery related:
shp.   Shaft Horse Power (steamers)   HP and LP- High and Low pressure turbines.
bhp.   Brake Horse Power (motor ships)
psi.   Pounds per square inch.   Kg/cm². Kilograms per square centimetre.
rpm.   Revolutions per minute
tpd.   Tons per day (fuel)
tph.   Tons per hour (pumps)   VLCC   Very Large Crude Carrier
m³/hr Cubic metres per hour.   OBO   Ore/Bulk/Oil type
H.O.   Heavy Fuel Oil   O/O   Ore/Oil carrier
D.O.   Diesel Oil   LPG   Liquefied Petroleum Gas type
FWE Finished with engines.   LNG   Liquefied Natural Gas type.
Kts.   Knots, speed in nautical miles (6,080ft.) per hour.   Reefer   Refrigerated Cargo Ship

Sundry measurements:
Anchor chain- 1 fathom = 6ft, 15 fathoms = 90ft = 1 shackle.
Stowage Factor- SF Cu.ft/long ton or m³/metric tonne for cargo commodity handled.
Long Tons to Metric Tonnes x 1.01605
1 Metre = 3.2808 ft.
1 Cubic Metre = 35.315 cu.ft.
1 US Barrel = 42 US Gallons, or 34.9726 Imperial Gallons.

Note- Many imperial measures were metricated during the period covered by this book – consequently certain
details per ship vary according to year of build. Some vessels were also re-measured in terms of tonnage
during their lifetime, following changes to International Loadline Regulations. Certain tonnages may seem at
variance to other sources.

Various forms of charter:-
Voyage Charter-
The ship's charterer pays the owner an agreed sum based on the tonnage of freight loaded. The shipowner
must then pay out all expenses involved in executing the voyage. A single, or sometimes consecutive voyages
may be covered in this way.

Time Charter-
The period of charter may be up to several years and the shipowner will be paid on the basis of summer
deadweight ton/month. He still has to pay all operating expenses including officers, crew, stores, provisions,
repair and maintenance, etc. However, the charterer will pay for bunkers and port expenses incurred.

Bareboat Charter-
The charterer pays an agreed amount to the shipowner and will in effect operate and man the vessel as if it
were his own, for the duration.

Demise Charter-
The provision of master, crew and maintenance of the ship still rests with the owner.
The charterer assumes all other operating costs and responsibilities.

INTRODUCTION and GENERAL BACKGROUND

Small quantities of vegetable and mineral oil had been transported by river and sea for centuries, generally shipped in barrels. In the latter part of the sailing ship era some built-in tank structural arrangements were attempted with varying degrees of success. In 1861, just two years after the first crude oil well in Philadelphia came on stream, the sailing brig Elizabeth Watts 224 tons, brought a cargo of oil in barrels to London for discharge. By 1878 a number of sailing ships had entered the trade and the infant bulk crude oil trade was not far away.

1. SS GLUCKAUF

Although not the very first steamer to be constructed for the bulk carriage of oil, this British built, German owned vessel has long been regarded as the 'forerunner' and prototype for modern tankers. Dating from 1886, she came off the slipways of the Newcastle firm of Armstrong Whitworth, to the order of the German-American Petroleum Company. The design surely held the blueprint for development. *Gluckauf* 2,307 grt/ 3,000 dwt measured 310ft x 37ft x 23ft.dr; her propulsion consisted of two 150 psi boilers providing steam for the triple expansion engines. A speed of 10kts could be achieved in service. The hull construction consisted of part iron, part steel and the design allowed for a central longitudinal bulkhead the length of the cargo spaces. This provided for eight pairs of cargo tanks with an expansion trunkway above each. A cargo pumproom and a coal bunker effectively formed the modern equivalent of a cofferdam, between cargo space and engine room. Every tanker today must by regulation have just such a space provided to isolate cargo from machinery areas. *Gluckauf* proved reliable in service but lasted only until 1893 when wrecked not far from New York.

In 1915 the British Tanker Company was formed to transport the products of the Anglo-Persian Oil Company. During WW1 the British owned, Eagle Oil Company was putting 17,000 ton tankers into service. Numbers in the trade similarly multiplied. By the 1920s ships of up to 20,000 tons had appeared, and from around 1925 the Norwegians entered the tanker market in what would become a continuous business to the present. The changeover from coal to oil fuel in industry and shipping accelerated between the two wars, with demand for crude oil undiminished to the present. WW2 saw a heavy and tragic loss of tankers and replacements could scarcely be built quickly enough.

This led to America's massive construction programme of standard cargo ships and tankers. Some 525 'T2' steam tankers were built between 1943-1945 and they would prove to be most durable and successful long after the war. The T2s were 523ft x 68ft x 30ft.dr in overall dimensions and powered by water tube boilers providing steam to turbo-electric machinery. Some 6,000 shp could be generated to give a service speed of 14.5 kts, although a number of more powerful variants were built. Some 16,000 tons of cargo could be carried and the cargo spaces were divided by a single central bulkhead in No.1 tank, but two fore and aft bulkheads in Nos.2-9 provided for a total of 26 tanks in all. There was a pumproom at both ends of the cargo space and a small dry cargo hold forward. Despite their wartime austerity image, many of these ships survived and served in the major oil company fleets through the 1950s and 1960s.

2.   SS ESSO BRISTOL (WW2 T2 type, b.1944, 10,712grt, ex SANDY CREEK) Post WW2 rebuilding and industrial expansion.

The immediate post WW2 period would see major rebuilding in Europe and the Far East together with general industrial expansion worldwide, yet at the same time there were new political uncertainties. A trend developed for oil refineries to be built at the consumer end of the supply chain, rather than producer. Additionally, several new major sources of crude oil were coming on stream leading to an ever growing ocean network of tanker routes. Another cause for the increase in tanker numbers would be the final changeover from coal to oil fuel for shipping in general. Some crude oil pipelines were built across the land mass from the Gulf to the Mediterranean to help ease the oil flow westwards, but in reality they were to prove vulnerable.

In 1956/7 the first Suez crisis erupted and the albeit brief Canal stoppage would be something of a wake up call for the future. It served to highlight the growing reliance placed by Western nations on a continuous supply of Middle East crude oil. From the UK or NW Europe the distance via Suez to the Gulf is, depending on ports, some 6,000 miles – or nearly three weeks steaming for a tanker. Via the Cape of Good Hope, South Africa, this is in excess of 11,500 miles requiring a steaming time of just over one month in each direction. Economically, this implied that a tanker might manage six laden, and six non-productive ballast voyages per year. In the 1950s a number of traditional British cargo liner and tramp ship companies decided to enter the expanding tanker market, thereby taking advantage of the expected continuing boom. The major oil companies continued to add tonnage to their fleets to satisfy demand, but for greater flexibility of operation it became commonplace for them to charter additional ships from outside owners. By the 1950s numerous 18,000 ton product tankers and 30,000 ton crude oil carriers were in service.

Such would be the impetus in the trade that by the 1960s 100,000 ton crude oil tankers were increasingly common in the search for economy of scale. Another giant leap in the 1970s saw 200,000 tonners multiplying in numbers – the VLCC had arrived! In 1967 the Middle East War erupted and serious long term disruption loomed for both cargo liners and oil tankers. This second Suez Canal stoppage was a far more serious affair than the first, as it would be some eight years before full reopening in 1975. For the duration all NW Europe – Mediterranean – Gulf – Far East traffic had an enforced diversion around South Africa. Cape Town became a major storing, bunkering and servicing centre, conveniently at about the half voyage point. Once the Canal re-opened there soon inevitably appeared a glut of many types of ship, with tankers being the worst affected. Leaner times had arrived for the ship owners in what always has been a 'boom or bust' industry.

The appearance and evolution of new ship types:-

LPG Carriers
The sea borne carriage of liquefied petroleum gas developed in the 1950s initially with the conversion of some small cargo coasters. The early system involved high pressure, ambient temperature cargo stowage in cylindrical tanks, not part of the ship's fixed structure. Specialist refrigerated gas (low pressure tank) carriers appeared from around 1953 but the type, size and numbers did not significantly develop until the 1960s and 1970s.

Chemical Tankers
Another post WW2 development would see tankers specially designed for the carriage of an ever increasing range of chemical products. These ships required systems far more sophisticated than oil tankers. Numbers multiplied as the use of plastics in the manufacturing industry grew.

LNG Carriers
The ocean transportation of Liquefied Natural Gas presented a far more onerous set of criteria and carriage problems. Liquid methane is carried at -161 degrees C in specialist tanks, containment and insulation systems, and it is common for the 'boil-off' of cargo on passage to be fed to the ship's boilers as fuel. The type evolved in the 1950s, was slow to develop in terms of ship numbers but today fleets of large LNG tankers are at work in several parts of the World. They are of necessity becoming more important again in the UK owing to the dwindling North Sea gas stocks.

Ore/Oil Carriers
In 1921 the first specialist O/O ship entered service and could carry oil in wing tanks on one voyage and iron ore in centre holds, on the next. By the 1950s Sweden had developed the type up to about 22,000 tons capacity. By the 1970s such craft had evolved technically and physically to above the 250,000 ton mark.

Ore/Bulk/Oil Carriers (OBOs)
This type proved to be very flexible indeed. The large central holds can be filled with crude oil to achieve a full deadweight. Depending on the stowage factor (SF) of the commodity involved, coal, grain or other dry bulk cargo may be similarly stowed to capacity. A full deadweight of dense iron ore may be achieved by loading alternate holds which are specially strengthened to accommodate such cargo against the enormous shearing forces involved. These ships have segregated wing and double bottom ballast tanks and special hold cleaning arrangements for the changeover from oil to dry cargo and vice versa.

Large Dry Bulk Carriers
Derived historically from traditional single deck cargo ships, these simply grew in size from the 1950s onward. Historically, at times of poor tanker freight rates, oil tankers had switched to the carriage of grain – the only dry bulk commodity for which they were suited. Specialist dry bulk carriers had arrived in great numbers by the 1970s, when they reached the 150,000 ton category. Coal, ores, grain, tapioca, scrap metal, in fact anything that can be spout or conveyor loaded and grab discharged, falls within their capability.

SECTION 1.

The P&O Group Board's decision in 1955 to 'enter the tanker market'
The original Group plan envisaged a fleet of steam tankers totalling some 500,000 tons deadweight. Orders were to be placed with the Company's traditional British shipyards and space allotted to build two classes of tanker. Firstly, a number of 18-19,000 ton range clean product tankers with the balance to be of 36-37,000 ton crude oil ships. These two size ranges were close to the industry optimum at the time. Delays in securing yard space and other external factors led to considerable deviation from the original plan. Fewer ships were ultimately built and individual sizes differed greatly from the 1955 plan, yet the total deadweight capacity of the fleet put into service between December 1958 and 1964 remained largely unaltered. The ships were initially lodged under the ownership of several P&O Group companies, some being managed by one of the others. The reasons appeared logical at the time, and were possibly connected with finance and tax allowances. A brief history of the individual companies now follows. Their earlier cargo interests are summarised for around 1960, as they came to grips with the new steam tanker management and operation.

British India Steam Navigation Company Ltd.
The title dates from 1862. However, it was founded in 1856 as the Calcutta and Burma Navigation Company Ltd, to carry mails for the East India Company. Other companies were acquired before the P&O amalgamation in 1914. Passenger and cargo services were:- UK/ Continent to Pakistan, India, Gulf, East Africa, Australia and a network of Indian Ocean services, also Australia-Japan. New tankers:- *Ellenga, Ellora, Queda* and *Talamba*.

Charter Shipping Company Ltd.(Bermuda)
A new company established by P&O themselves in order to operate their own tankers.
New tankers:- *Maloja*, *Mantua*, *Malwa*, *Foyle* (later renamed *Megna* and managed by James Nourse Ltd; *Derby* (managed by Federal).

Federal Steam Navigation Company Ltd.
Constituted in 1895, the origins were with Money, Wigram a sailing ship company with origins in the eighteenth century. This had been the source of the cross of St.George on the company flag and later funnel emblem. The rectangular blue panel was added to the centre of the flag in 1763 following objections from the Royal Navy. Federal merged with the New Zealand Shipping Company in 1912, becoming part of P&O in 1916. Services:- UK/USA – Australia / New Zealand via Panama. New tankers:- *Kent*, *Lincoln*.

Hain Steamship Company Ltd.
Established at St.Ives, Cornwall in 1833 by Edward Hain, the fleet consisted of sailing vessels until the first tramp steamer was acquired in 1878. The steamers had taken over before P&O acquired the company in 1917. In 1965 Hain merged with James Nourse in order to operate the new bulk carriers then coming into service. Hain-Nourse would continue this function until the 1971 P&O Group re-organisation. There were no directly owned tankers.

Moss Hutchison Line, Ltd; Liverpool.
This company had resulted from the 1934 merger of James Moss & Co. Ltd (Moss Line) whose origins went back to 1860, with J&P Hutchison from 1850. General Steam Navigation acquired the firms in 1935 and thus they became part of the P&O Group. The services were mainly cargo from UK/NW Europe to the Mediterranean and Black Seas. New tanker:- *Busiris* (managed by B.I.S.N.Co.Ltd.).

New Zealand Shipping Company Ltd.
Began in Christchurch, New Zealand in 1873 and incorporated the New Zealand Freight Company and a crack fleet of sailing ships. In 1882 NZS brought the first ever consignment of frozen meat from New Zealand to the United Kingdom. In 1912 the firm merged with the Federal Steam Navigation Company and control passed to P&O in 1916. Services were:- mail/passengers/cargo UK/Continent – Panama Canal – New Zealand. Also East Coast USA/Canada to Australia/New Zealand. New tanker:- *Quiloa* (Managed by B.I.S.N.Co.Ltd).

James Nourse Ltd.
Established in 1861, a fleet of some twenty sailing ships were gradually replaced by steamers from around 1903. Passenger and cargo services:- Calcutta/Rangoon to the West Indies and Cuba via the Cape of Good Hope, and the UK. The Company became part of P&O by 1917. Tanker:- *Erne*.

Orient Steam Navigation Company Ltd.
Its history went back to 1797 when James Thompson & Co became established as shipowners. By 1850 they were running the Orient Line of clipper ships to Australia. In 1863 the firm became known as Anderson, Thompson & Co, thence Anderson, Anderson & Co in 1869. In 1878 together with Frederick Green & Co, the Orient Steam Navigation Company was formed to run steamers to Australia. Brothers Richard and Henry Green were builders of the celebrated 'Blackwall frigates'. There had been an early link with the Pacific Steam Navigation Company of Liverpool, regarding ship chartering. P&O took over the Orient Steam Navigation Company in December 1918. Services:- passenger and cargo London – Mediterranean – Suez –Aden – Colombo – to Australian ports. Also cruising. Tanker:- *Garonne*.

Peninsular and Oriental Steam Navigation Company.
It started before 1837 in the Iberian Peninsula trade to Spain and Portugal, with an eye on expansion eastwards. There were seven steamers in the fleet in that year. In 1843 the first steamer was based at Suez for onward service to Calcutta. Passengers and mails had of course to be transported by land across Egypt. The opening of the Suez Canal in 1869 would see a proliferation of direct through services from Europe to the East. Services:- Passengers/cargo London/UK – Far East via Suez. Sydney – Far East – West Coast USA; and cruising. Tankers:- see Charter Shipping Company, above.

The Trident Tanker era, 1962-1971.

As the fleet of new steam tankers began operating under their various P&O Group Companies, it soon became apparent that efficiencies and economies could be made if all such factions merged into a single entity. A central operating body would also be better placed to deal with the tanker 'market place'. The formation of Trident Tankers Ltd in December 1962 soon made just such a plan reality. The diversely liveried ships were quickly given a new corporate makeover of black hulls, with stone coloured upper works, topped off with a plain black funnel bearing a white diamond, complete with black trident. By 1967 three new motor tankers and the company's first motor OBOs were in service. Experience was rapidly gained by both sea staff and shore staff in the operation of ever more technically advanced vessels. A true new company identity quickly formulated, leading to the industry perception of a good quality operation for the newcomer.

By 1967 the overall capacity of the fleet neared 1,000,000 tons, making Trident the largest independent UK tanker owner and operator – in just five years. In 1970 the four giant 214,000 ton 'Ard' class tankers entered service with long term charters to major oil companies. On the personnel level, seagoing officers and crew alike wore uniforms and boiler suits distinguished with Company badges, buttons and insignia. For those ashore, a plain black company tie adorned with small 'tridents' could be purchased. A quarterly house-magazine, 'Trident Topics' was circulated around the fleet – and appreciated, as it always contained an updated fleet personnel list. As with the parent company, P&O, Trident always actively encouraged training through the ranks from deck and engineering cadets to fully qualified senior positions. Within a remarkably short number of years a not inconsiderable company loyalty evolved – not something generally much evidenced in industry today.

The early tankers will now be looked at in detail.

3.   SS LINCOLN

Laden and looking smart in the new Trident livery is the P&O Group's first ocean going tanker. Built by John Brown of Clydebank, she was delivered in December 1958 to the Federal Steam Navigation Company and would not come directly under Trident control until January 1964. The ship would seem not to have been a great success as she lasted in the fleet only until 1965. In essence the design had changed but little from the war time standard of the T2s, with the exception of some minor streamlining and doubtless more advanced accommodation. The dimensions of product tankers barely altered during the 1950s and 1960s – allowing access to most ports around the World for the distribution of clean, refined oil products. This vessel measured 558ft 03in x 72ft. x 30ft.dr. with tonnages of 12,780grt and 18,500dwt. Two water tube boilers supplied superheated steam at 800deg.F and 610psi to steam turbines, double reduction geared to a single propeller shaft. Two steam generators provided for the electrical load. Two cargo pumprooms were fitted, one below the foredeck between cargo tanks and similarly, one below the main deck.

4. SS GARONNE

The photograph is seen courtesy of ©P&O Heritage Collection (DP World). This steam tanker had the distinction of being the first of the Group's larger class of crude oil carriers when delivered in December 1959 by Vickers of Newcastle. *Garonne* measured 24,513grt and 37,000dwt with dimensions of 690ft.06in. x 90ft.05in. x 37ft.10in.dr. Propulsion again would be provided by steam turbines producing 16,000 shp at 105rpm, giving a speed of 16.5kts. The ship entered service under the Orient Steam Navigation Co. before transfer to Trident in 1963. She was sold out of the Group in 1973. The initial Orient 'corn' colour hull livery, similar to their passenger liners, seems singularly inappropriate for a crude oil tanker, and the change to black hull and funnel could probably not have come quickly enough.

5. SS ELLORA

Built for the British India Steam Navigation Co. by Swan Hunter and Wigham Richardson at Wallsend, this ship entered service in May 1960. She would be managed by Trident from August 1963 until sold in 1970. Of 24,500grt and 37,140dwt her dimensions were virtually the same as for No.4. In the photograph the original British India funnel marking of two white rings close together has been replaced by the new 'Trident' motif. Seen in ballast, the ship's immaculate appearance indicates ex drydock condition.

6.   SS MALOJA

Owned by the Charter Shipping Company (Bermuda), this product tanker would be initially managed by P&OS.N.Co, from September 1959 until Trident took her over in 1964. Built by Smiths Dock, Middlesbrough she measured 12,763grt, 19,948dwt on dimensions of 559ft. 03in. x 71ft.05in. x 30ft.11in.dr. Again the chosen power unit consisted of a set of steam turbines providing a laden speed of 14.75kts and 15.25kts in ballast. Two Foster Wheeler ESD Boilers supplied steam at 800deg.F. and 530psi on a fuel consumption of 53tpd. Four turbine driven, centrifugal type cargo pumps rated at 468tph each at 1,200rpm, handled the cargo discharges along with a single steam stripping pump housed in an after pumproom. In common with many tankers of the day, one 10 inch cargo discharge line was fitted at the stern for use in Mediterranean ports where mooring stern on to the quay was by no means unusual.

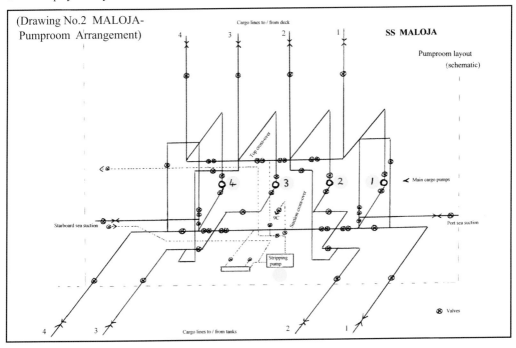

7.   SS MALOJA (Manchester Ship Canal)

With the industrial backdrop of Ellesmere Port up ahead, *Maloja* is en route to the giant Stanlow Oil Refinery on the Manchester Ship Canal in this 1976 photograph. This size of tanker was right on the maximum dimensions allowed to percolate above Eastham Locks from the River Mersey. Ships of this size could not proceed further inland towards Manchester. One of the Canal Company's many tugs can just be seen leading the way on the ship's bow in this view from the monkey island.

8.   SS DERBY

Despite the early Federal Steam Navigation livery, this crude oil tanker's owner was Charter Shipping. Federal managed this vessel through until 1966 when she briefly passed to Trident. *Derby* and sister vessel *Kent* never lost their Federal funnel colours until sold in 1968. Delivered in May 1960 by John Brown, Clydebank, *Derby* at 31,791grt and 48,884dwt on dimensions of 759ft. x 98ft x 40ft.dr., was indeed a large tanker of the day. She could manage 16.25kts service speed and judging by the image taken off the Kent Coast, must have been brand new or just drydocked at the time. For more technical details see No.10.

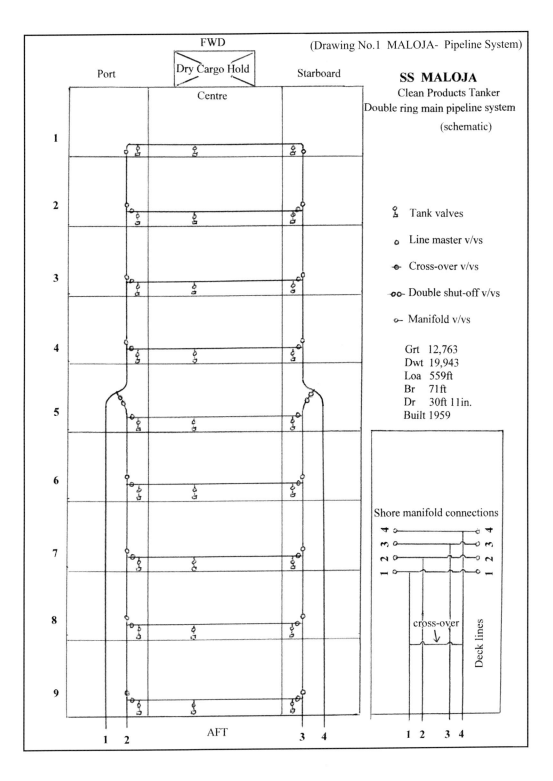

FWD

Port

Dry Cargo Hold

Starboard

Centre

(Drawing No.1 MALOJA- Pipeline System)

SS MALOJA
Clean Products Tanker
Double ring main pipeline system
(schematic)

Tank valves

Line master v/vs

Cross-over v/vs

Double shut-off v/vs

Manifold v/vs

Grt   12,763
Dwt 19,943
Loa   559ft
Br   71ft
Dr   30ft 11in.
Built 1959

Shore manifold connections

cross-over

Deck lines

AFT

9.   SS ELLENGA

Sister vessel to *Ellora* this tanker was delivered from Swan Hunter in May 1960 for the British India Steam Navigation Co. She passed into Trident in August 1963 remaining in the fleet until sold on in 1970. Of the '37,000'ton crude oil carrier class, her main machinery and physical dimensions were a repeat of Nos.4&5.

10. SS KENT

From the same Clydebank Shipyard as sister vessel *Derby*, this ship entered service in December 1960 for Federal Steam Navigation. Similarly, she would also only be under Trident operation from 1966 to 1968 when sold. Both ships were powered by double reduction geared steam turbines producing 18,000shp by way of a 21ft diam. propeller weighing 29 tons, 5 cwt. The light ship 'steelwork' amounted to 16,429tons. Cargo discharge equipment consisted of four Drysdale turbine driven centrifugal pumps rated at 1,380tph each. Drainage was accomplished by two vertical duplex stripping pumps rated at 330tph. Unusually advanced for their day these tankers had a good percentage of space segregated for clean ballast water. Also, a system of remote cargo tank gauging 'teledep' was fitted. An additional small midships pumproom housed two 300tph ballast pumps for the segregated system. In the aerial photograph the ship has yet to acquire the more practical black hull colour, far better suited to the crude oil trade.

Breakdown of ship types in service

	1964	Feb-74	Feb-74	Mar-83	Mid 1994	Notes:
Product Tankers	6 (0)	3 (2)		3 (0)		
Crude Oil Tankers	10 (3)	10 (1)		2 (0)		
Bulk Carriers		4 (1)		3 (0)	10 +	+ plus similar number chartered in
LPG Tankers		4 (2)(1)		9 + 1*		* includes one LNG Carrier
Ore/Bulk/Oil Carriers		6 (0)		3 (0)		
Ore/Oil Carriers		1 (0)				
Passenger/Cargo Ships			3 (0)			
Cargo Ships			46 (6)			
Refrigerated Cargo Ships			25 (1)	5 (0)		
Container Ships			8 <>			<> 4 of which, managed for OCL
Totals-	16 (3)	28 (7)	82 (7)	26 (0)	10 (0)	
	Trident	P&O BSD	P&O GCD	DSCD	P&O BSL	
					P&O BCL	

Notes:

(2) indicates two ships on order

+ plus similar number chartered in

* includes one LNG Carrier

<> 4 of which, managed for OCL

Trident Tankers Ltd
P&O Bulk Shipping Division
"   General Cargo Division
"   Deep Sea Cargo Division
"   Bulk Shipping Limited
"   Bulk Carriers Limited

The 1964 list shows the early Trident Tanker expanding fleet although gas carriers were some years ahead.

The 1974 part one list shows expansion into gas carrying and dry bulk together with the OBO & O/O types.

The 1974 part two list shows the Group's rationalised cargo fleet as it faced containerisation of ocean trades.

The 1983 list marks a major reduction in oil tanker operation and near demise of the Group's traditional cargo ships.

The 1994 list shows only involvement in large dry bulk carrier shipping.

11. SS KENT Forward to Midships

At sea in 1966, and the view from the bow top clearly shows two anchor capstans rather than the more common windlasses. Midships bridge structure type tankers were still being built in some numbers up to about 1960. The midships accommodation for the Master, Deck Officers, Radio Officer, Chief Steward and one Steward was largely free of noise and vibration, and the loudest sound would often be that of the air conditioning unit blowers.

12. SS KENT Midships to Aft

The Chief Engineer, all Engineering Officers and the Crew lived in the after accommodation 'close to the job'. However as all galley and catering arrangements were situated 'down aft', it was the Deck Department who had to brave bad weather along the flying bridge to reach their meals. Conversely, since the Officers' bar was amidships, the traffic went into reverse for recreational purposes.

13. SS KENT Aft to Midships

Completing the tour, here we see the Engineers' view of the midships Navigators' domain. The four main deck cargo pipelines from the pumproom running to the shore connection manifolds beneath the pair of hose handling derricks are clearly visible. The small 'bus stop' shelters along the catwalk were vital protection in heavy weather laden condition, as seas tend to march across tankers' decks. Good judgement of the waves and rolling of the ship did not always lead to a 'dry' arrival at the other end!

14. SS KENT Federal Tankers - funnel insignia

Bright red with a black top, Federal's white flag and red St.George's cross carried a central blue rectangular panel. *Kent & Derby* were never fully assimilated into the Trident fleet in terms of livery, but they did eventually acquire a stylish 'FT' emblem on the funnel flag implying Federal Tankers, for their last couple of years' service.

15. Suez Canal (Southbound lay-by)

Taken from the stern of *Kent* in April 1966, a number of tankers in ballast are moored in line to the Canal lay-by bank, during a Southbound convoy on route to the Gulf. They would remain here for a few hours whilst deeply laden tankers and other types passed northwards a mile or so to the East, on the main Canal off to the right of the photograph.

16. SS MANTUA

Seen here anchored of Southend Pier awaiting orders, and right at the end of her career in 1976, is the sister vessel to *Maloja*. The builders were Smith's Dock who delivered her in October 1960 to Charter Shipping. In 1964 she came under Trident control. The ship's tonnages were 12,752grt, 19,859dwt and in most other details bore a great similarity to the sister vessel, with one major difference. *Mantua* had one additional midships accommodation deck. These two ships closely resembled Shell's 'A' class product tankers, and would spend their working lives demise chartered to that Company. With a small laden motor coaster heading towards London, *Mantua's* anchor cable is 'up and down' indicating slack water.

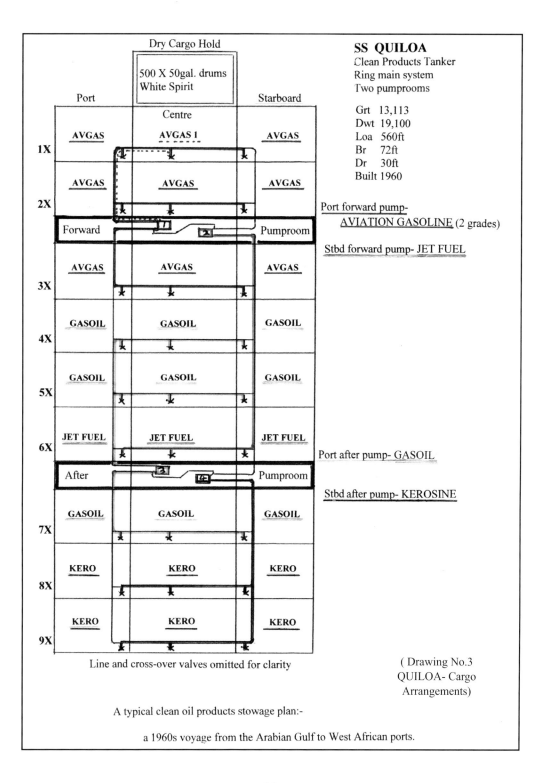

Dry Cargo Hold

500 X 50gal. drums
White Spirit

SS QUILOA
Clean Products Tanker
Ring main system
Two pumprooms

Port	Centre	Starboard	

Grt 13,113
Dwt 19,100
Loa 560ft
Br 72ft
Dr 30ft
Built 1960

	Port	Centre	Starboard
1X	AVGAS	AVGAS 1	AVGAS
2X	AVGAS	AVGAS	AVGAS
	Forward		Pumproom
3X	AVGAS	AVGAS	AVGAS
4X	GASOIL	GASOIL	GASOIL
5X	GASOIL	GASOIL	GASOIL
6X	JET FUEL	JET FUEL	JET FUEL
	After		Pumproom
7X	GASOIL	GASOIL	GASOIL
8X	KERO	KERO	KERO
9X	KERO	KERO	KERO

Port forward pump-
    AVIATION GASOLINE (2 grades)

Stbd forward pump- JET FUEL

Port after pump- GASOIL

Stbd after pump- KEROSINE

Line and cross-over valves omitted for clarity

(Drawing No.3
QUILOA- Cargo
Arrangements)

A typical clean oil products stowage plan:-

a 1960s voyage from the Arabian Gulf to West African ports.

17. SS QUILOA

Curiously, this steam product tanker also had one sister vessel with an additional midships deck, *Queda*. These two were both built at Scott's Greenock Yard on the Clyde. *Queda* was placed under British India ownership and passed into Trident control in June 1963. She was sold to Peru in 1969 and reportedly converted to an LPG carrier before scrapping in 1981. Returning to the photograph subject, *Quiloa* was placed under New Zealand Shipping Co. ownership initially, but would be under British India management until Trident control in 1963. The ship's statistics were 13,113grt, 19,943dwt on dimensions of 560ft. x 72ft. x 30ft.dr. Two pumprooms were fitted each with duplex steam cargo pumps and a stripping pump, in the old style. A dry cargo hold forward served by a derrick permitted the carriage of dry goods such as case oil or drums, as required for many remote outport destinations with a lack of facilities. In this July 1969 photograph, the ship is completing discharge at the remote Ango Ango wharf some seventy five miles from the sea up the River Congo. This isolated berth was situated a few miles downstream from Matadi, the head of navigation for sea-going vessels. Not such a common operation even by 1969, the fore hold derrick had just unloaded drum cargo into a barge alongside. The voyage up from the sea had been completely uneventful, but in the rainy season 10 knot currents can bring entire 'islands' of floating vegetation downstream!

18. SS QUILOA at Durban

On one return West Africa voyage around the Cape of Good Hope to the Gulf, a serious mechanical problem arose when the ship was just a few miles off Durban. A thermometer pocket on the HP turbine casing collapsed into the rotor, wrecking the blades. In this 1969 photograph the ship has been berthed in Durban harbour for assessment of repairs and removal of the turbine rotor. Since the ship had completed tank cleaning and gas freeing some days earlier, she was unusually 'double berthed' against a cargo vessel for a few days. (Livanos Group's *PEARL TRADER*). A floating harbour crane removed the offending turbine complete, and after steam pipe and other modifications were completed, the ship duly sailed on LP turbine power only, at reduced speed. It took some months before a new HP rotor could be built and subsequently replaced at the next dry docking. In the photograph, the open door just beneath the lifeboat deck was the Mates' cargo office. Centralised cargo control rooms had yet to appear, and the cargo pumps were started and stopped by telephone to the engine room from a gauge panel at the top of the pumproom. Tachometers indicated pump revolutions and the main cargo pumps could be slowed from 1300rpm to 900rpm for tank drainage purposes – simple but very effective.

19. SS QUILOA at Venice

Passing through Venice in June 1970 on route to Porto Marghera, the industrial part, the ship was due to load a part cargo of Gasoil for West Germany. The fore, and after deck pumproom top vent cowls can be clearly seen. Your Author was on watch at the time and had reached the dizzy rank of 3rd Officer! The backdrop needs no description.

20. River Weser tank barges →

The cargo mentioned in No.19 duly went ashore at Brake on the German River Weser, much of it discharged directly into river tank barges alongside. In this photograph, three of the immaculately kept craft lie alongside the ship. The middle barge Patria looks different as she appears to have accommodation at each end, with the wheelhouse in the middle.

21. SS QUILOA's chart table →

Prior to the advent of 'satnav' satellite navigation systems, the old tried and trusted method of navigation reigned supreme. Sextant, Nautical Almanac, Star Tables, Burton's or Norie's Nautical Tables and a reliable chronometer for GMT were essential ingredients. Of course the Decca Navigation System of hyperbolic radio wave lattices printed onto the charts was in common use for coastal navigation, but not too many ships in the fifties or sixties had the ocean 'Loran' system fitted. Celestial navigation had evolved over the centuries and provided that a reasonable DR (dead reckoning) position was known, plus GMT, then at twilight night and morning star sights could be taken to work out the ship's real position. Heavenly bodies and the horizon have to be clearly visible to obtain the vital sextant angle to proceed with the calculations. Mid morning by tradition the 3rd and 2nd Mates both took a couple of sun sights, the position lines resulting from which, would be run up ahead on the plotting chart, to be used at noon when a sight of the sun as it crossed the meridian, yielded a latitude. The resultant noon 'fix' would then be used to calculate the day's distance run, average speed for 24 hours and the voyage, fuel consumed and remaining, plus the estimated time of arrival (eta) at the next port, etc.

22. SS QUILOA radar and steering position

Looking from starboard to port across *Quiloa's* wheelhouse, just visible far left is the ship's metal steering wheel and auto-pilot position. By 1970 traditional wooden steering wheels were well and truly outmoded, as a move to miniaturise had begun in earnest. The gyro compass read-out is perched atop the steering console, and overhead a traditional periscope read-out for the ship's magnetic compass sited above on the monkey island, can be seen in the event of gyro failure. Nearest the camera the bulk of the Decca TM829 radar set is visible. This early true-motion radar was a great advance technically, as instead of the ship always remaining at the centre of the rotating scan line, speed could be fed into the set, and the ship therefore moved across the screen whilst the land appeared static. The true courses of other vessels could now be seen at a glance.

23. SS QUILOA in Falmouth Drydock →

Vast quantities of weed and barnacles were removed at this 1970 drydocking. Trading in the tropics at low speed on reduced power whilst awaiting the rebuild of the HP turbine had caused such phenomenal growth (see No.18). Note the use of traditional wooden 'shores' to keep the vessel upright on the blocks. Falmouth drydocks, part of the P&O Group itself from 1918 until 1977, had not long since ceased using steam shunting engines on the yard site. The railed steam cranes were still trundling around doing odd jobs about the place.

24. SS BUSIRIS ↘

Delivered by Thompson's yard at Sunderland in February 1961, this crude oil tanker was another in the 37,000dwt series, and she would be owned by Moss Hutchison, yet managed by British India. She passed to Trident control in April 1963 and was eventually sold for further trading in July 1976. *Busiris* was demise chartered to Shell. Her dimensions were much the same as the others in the class, and following re-measurement for the new Load Line Regulations her

dead-weight rose to 39,288 tons. A speed of 15.5kts laden and 16.5kts in ballast could be achieved on a consumption of 91tpd of fuel oil. The class all had similar cargo handling equipment, namely 4 x 1,350tph centrifugal, steam turbine driven cargo pumps and 2 x 330tph steam stripping pumps. Steam heating coils were fitted in all cargo tanks for the heavier grades. Two Foster Wheeler ESD boilers provided steam at 850degF/600psi to a set of geared turbines giving 16,000shp at 105rpm. In the photograph the ship is looking very smart having possibly just acquired the Trident livery.

25. SS MALWA

Around the year 1960 a trend developed in shipbuilding whereby the midships bridge structure, common to nearly all previous oil tankers, would be placed aft. At the time a considerable body of opinion united against any such radical design change, on the basis of extended bow shadow generated. Perceived wisdom led to the belief that this 'blind spot' would cause serious mayhem in crowded waters. No such real difficulties arose however, but it would be some years before the midships design passed into history. Of course, there were immense benefits from housing everyone aft, not least from the safety angle – you no longer lived over the top of the cargo! Also savings in domestic plumbing and wiring arrangements could be made, along with rationalised lifeboat positions. One minor disadvantage noted by the Deck Department was the greater vibration and engine noise, inevitable at the after end. Invariably the old steamers suffered far less from the problem than the later motor ships. However today, detailed studies are undertaken by vibration specialists at the design stage, to try to alleviate the problems. *Malwa* came from the Vickers yard at Barrow-in-Furness in November 1961, and despite looking so different in profile was actually another standard dimensions ship, in the 37,000dwt series. Her owners were Charter Shipping and managers P&OS.N.Co., before transferring to Trident in July 1963. Her original statistics were 24,300grt and 37,278dwt but the latter increased to 39,295dwt following re-measurement. She could manage a speed of 16.25kts on 92tpd at 16,000shp/105rpm. The lightship weight was 11,425tons. In the photograph she sports a rather curiously shaped funnel top extension provided soon after entering service, as the original short 'motor ship' type funnel failed to clear boiler uptake soot away from deck areas. The white diamond with 'trident' has been painted just above the original funnel top level. Charter Shipping's funnels were typical P&O plain black, but a short lived embellishment when new, was the application of a white or stone coloured band right around the hull at main deck level, as carried by P&O cargo liners of the same period. Crew numbers were still high when this ship came into service as little or no automation had appeared, and the fact is well illustrated in the photograph by the provision of four lifeboats – the midships pair have simply been moved aft to fit the new design.

26. SS MALWA at Nynashamn, Sweden →

Here the ship is unloading North African crude oil at a refinery south of Stockholm in July 1966. The Baltic Sea did not feature very often in the Company ships' voyages. *Malwa* was on charter to BP at the time and of course went wherever instructed.

27. SS MALWA - a single hose discharge ↘

Discharge here would have taken nearer a couple of days with just one hose provided, but on rare occasions when this happened it did afford more of the Officers and Crew a little time when off-duty, for a good run ashore. Oil tanker port 'turnarounds' are generally hectic affairs with cargo required to be off-loaded within twenty four hours, given full pumping ability.

28. Native dugouts, Bonny, Nigeria

The North West Europe to Bonny, Nigeria run regularly occupied a number of tankers in the 1960s. It involved around a twelve day sea passage each way, and the ballast leg gave good time for tank cleaning and maintenance jobs. Bonny Terminal consisted of a couple of buoy-berths off the river bank and facilities were quite rudimentary. The photograph taken from *Malwa's* poop deck in March 1966 shows a group of local bumboats, dug-out canoes peddling their wares alongside. They were usually well stocked with bananas, pineapples, coconuts and other local produce which could be bartered for with just about anything, except cash. The whole process was frowned upon by officialdom, but as long as the boatmen stayed off the ship, everyone turned a blind eye. There were, however, a few transactions which would soon be banned by international regulation, concerning the carriage of certain creatures deemed to be pets, back to Europe. This might involve African Grey parrots or even the odd tiny monkey. Sadly, few of the parrots survived the trip, as cold air conditioned cabins were a poor substitute for their normal tropical environment.

30. SS FOYLE →

Although built for Charter Shipping ownership, this traditional style crude oil tanker went under James Nourse Ltd management. She came from Connells' shipyard in Glasgow in February 1961 and transferred to Trident in 1964. Shortly afterwards in 1965 and probably in the interests of standardisation, she was renamed *Megna* thereby matching Charter Shipping's other 'M' names. In technical detail the ship differed little from the earlier 37,000 tonners already described.

29. An off-shore 'sea berth', Ivory Coast

This scene from the 1960s is included to highlight the difference between the lives of tanker men and their cargo ship counterparts. Abidjan, on the Ivory Coast in West Africa sounds like a splendid place for a run ashore, and indeed the cargo ships would tie up in port for several days at a time. However, this tanker berth was some three miles out to sea, with no shore leave permitted at all! The ship's derrick has been raised to heave the submarine oil pipeline clear of the sea bed, so that loading can commence. The stern was moored to buoys whilst the bow remained in position only by the ship's own anchors and cables.

31. SS ERNE

The trend towards the 'all aft' look manifested itself again in February 1962 when this new profile product tanker left Connells' yard at Glasgow. James Nourse were the owners and she transferred to Trident in May 1963 operationally, but not until 1969 for ownership. In 1970 after eight years in the clean products trade, *Erne* became bare boat chartered to BPNZ and had cargo heating modifications installed ready for the bitumen trade around the coast of New Zealand. Special helical heating coils enabled the bitumen to be kept in fluid state and the ship's steam plant undoubtedly proved ideal for this function. Although very slightly larger than the earlier product carriers in terms of tonnage, the overall dimensions remained the same. Of 13,728grt, 20,090dwt and 560ft x 72ft. x 31ft.dr., with steam turbine power she could manage 14.5kts on 53tpd fuel consumption. Another probable reason for the choice of this ship for the bitumen trade was the type of cargo pumps fitted. Two steam reciprocating pumps rated at 500tph each and a stripping pump rated at 60tph, were repeated in two pumprooms. In the photograph from the 1960s, it is evident that as was the case with *Malwa*, the funnel proved of insufficient height for the job. This ship has had a simple uptake extension pipe installed, rather than major funnel modifications.

32. SS ERNE,
Manila Anchorage, Philipines. →

In 1984 the ship's New Zealand operators brought in a new replacement tanker for their special trade, and the *Erne*, which seemed to have become something of an icon on the Kiwi Coast, redelivered to P&O when the charter terminated. The New Zealand Master, officers and crew remained as part of the deal to take the ship to Manila for tank cleaning, and thence on to Taiwan to the scrapyard. In this photo the old ship has reached Manila anchorage ready to receive the labour required to render the tanks clean and gas free for hot work – the cutter's torch. All traces of oil or gas must of necessity be eliminated before the Chemist will issue his Certificate. The cold deposit of bitumen proved something of a problem – removal only by pick axe and shovel! The ship had been exceptionally well maintained during her fourteen years trading around New Zealand, and in the photograph still carries the 'silver fern' motif on the funnel. Upon re-delivery to P&O it was impossible to find further work for her since modern motor tankers of similar dimensions would consume only half the fuel – a modest 25-30tpd instead of 53tpd. She must have been one of the best maintained vessels ever to go for scrap!

33. SS ERNE Catwalk and maindeck →

Compared to larger tankers, the deck appears very cluttered indeed. This ship could rival some cargo ships in the derricks status – no less than five being present. One right forward to work the dry cargo hold, two amidships for hose handling, and finally two at the break of the accommodation for stores handling, etc. Wire stays were still white lead and tallow coated in the time honoured manner.

34. SS ERNE Bridge
to forecastle

All tank lids are open for ventilation and the tanks have been gas freed. During the following days a considerable quantity of solid bitumen was dug, bagged, lifted and removed from the ship by barge, thanks to the efforts of the local work squad.

35. SS ERNE
New Zealand charter funnel →

Close observation of this photograph shows the two raised rings around the funnel where the original James Nourse markings were once painted. Also just discernible by the silver fern emblem is the edge of the Trident diamond – the ship's three different working phases all still visible right through to the Far East scrapyard.

36. VLCC scrapyard →

This scene dates from 1984 in the legendary Taiwan scrapyard at Kaohsiung, and the little *Erne* is being unceremoniously shunted astern by tugs between some of the World's largest redundant VLCCs. Visible left to right are *Turquoise*, *Norbega*, *Avin Oil Leader* and finally the ex Norwegian, *Kong Haakon VII*. All of these ships were around half the age of the *Erne*, yet surplus to oil industry requirements.

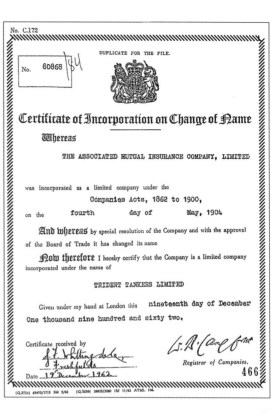

37. 'F.W.E.' ERNE's last movement.

Still looking in all respects ready to load the next cargo, the ship's final resting place has been reached amongst the giants and the boilers blown down. The same cutter's torch fate awaits all.

38. The scrapman awaits →

The shore derricks await to lift chunks of 'dead' ship ashore, and the old cargo vessel astern of *Erne* has already lost some masts and gear. Short work will be made of the remainder.

39. SS TALAMBA →

Delivered by Swan Hunter in February 1964, this ship marks the beginning of the trend towards larger vessels for Trident. She was built for the British India Steam Navigation Company and was originally to have been named *Erinpura*. She would be operated by Trident and then Bulk Shipping Division, until her untimely demise in early 1976 when out in the North Atlantic on passage from North Africa to Texas with crude oil. A main condenser sea water pipe fractured causing major flooding to the engine room. In the true tradition of seafarers in time of crisis, a table tennis table top was swiftly commandeered to stem the flow! Initially the ship was towed to the Azores for assessment and later onwards to Brest. Repairs proved uneconomical as damage to the engine room was severe and the ship's age against her. A Hamburg scrapyard eventually did the necessary deed a few months later. The ship's details were - 34,479grt and 54,000dwt, but this latter figure later rose to 59,820dwt upon re-measurement. Her propulsion unit consisted of two Babcock and Wilcox selectable super heated boilers providing steam at 850degF/600psi to a set of geared turbines. Some 17,600shp could be produced at 105rpm to give a speed of 15.25kts with a consumption of 92tpd. Quite advanced in one respect, the ship had an inert gas plant fitted in order to blanket the atmosphere above the cargo, or when tanks were empty or being cleaned. Boiler flue gases were passed through a scrubbing tower to remove sooty particulate matter, before being piped to →

the cargo spaces. All cargo tanks were fitted with steam heating coils for the heavier grades of cargo. The main cargo pumps consisted of four x 1,350tph centrifugal steam driven units. One similar capacity ballast pump was fitted along with two 330tph Dorman, Downey steam stripping pumps for tank drainage. The ship's overall dimensions were 765ft. 06in. x 105ft. 05in. x 41ft.dr. The unusual two funnel design had become popular with a number of owners – P&O's passenger liner *Canberra* had entered service not long before!

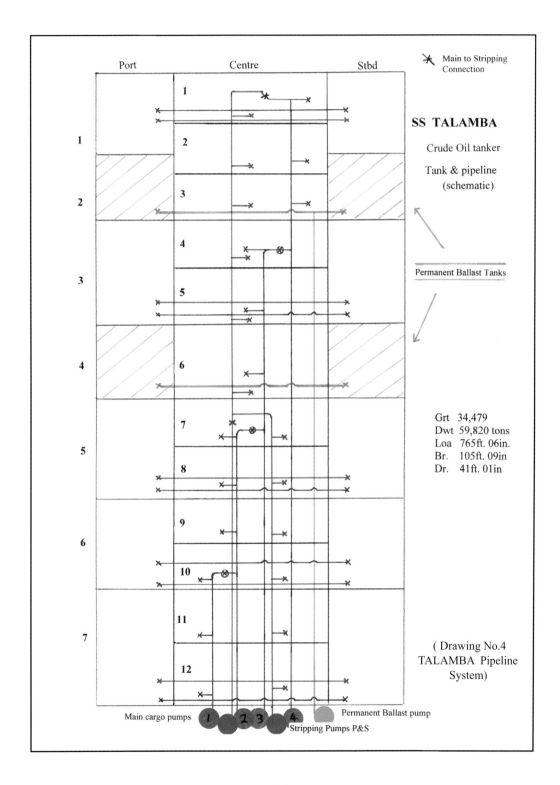

Port   Centre   Stbd

⚹ Main to Stripping Connection

SS TALAMBA

Crude Oil tanker

Tank & pipeline (schematic)

Permanent Ballast Tanks

Grt   34,479
Dwt 59,820 tons
Loa   765ft. 06in.
Br.   105ft. 09in
Dr.   41ft. 01in

(Drawing No.4 TALAMBA Pipeline System)

Main cargo pumps   1 2 3 4   Permanent Ballast pump
Stripping Pumps P&S

40. SS TALAMBA Cape Town

With the lengthy closure of the Suez Canal due to the Middle East War, Cape Town in particular, and Durban benefited from a huge increase in daily ship visits. All kinds of vessels making the enforced long passage around the Cape of Good Hope required fuel, water, stores, and

repairs. In this 1967 scene, *Talamba* is in ballast on route from Germany to the Gulf and the long sea passage was a bonus for maintenance to be carried out – especially in the cleaned and gas freed cargo tanks. With Lion Mountain ahead and the usual 'table cloth' on top of Table Mountain, the ship awaits the Agent's launch. The derrick is ready to bring aboard any urgently needed spares, fresh produce, a consignment of mail, a box or two of films, and on the odd occasion an exchange Seafarers Education Service Library. At the halfway point of the month long voyage, mail from home would be most keenly awaited.

41. Bunkering, Cape Verde Islands

Given standard sailing orders from the Gulf, *Talamba* headed around South Africa and onwards towards L.E.F.O. (Land's End for orders) – a term well known by all tankermen. This would normally imply a final discharge port somewhere in North West Europe, the United Kingdom or the Mediterranean Sea area. Late in 1967 when steaming Northwards in the South Atlantic, orders were received to proceed to the USA port of Portland, Maine. Additional bunkers were vital so a deviation to the Cape Verde Islands followed, to remedy the situation. In the photograph the tiny Cardiff registered steam tug *John Miller* 40grt/1937 is bringing out one of two rather venerable looking bunker barges to complete the job. The tug belonged to Millers and Cory (C.V.I.) Ltd; she had been built at Lytham.

42. Heavy weather, Western Atlantic

Following the bunker call the ship spent a number of days battling severe weather on route to Portland, Maine. The winds had moderated after a December gale, but a very heavy and irregular swell prevailed. Decks were continually awash for days on end yet fortunately no serious damage occurred, and it was something of a fluke to capture this photograph. *Talamba*, although on reduced speed because of the conditions, had just managed to find a 'hole' in the ocean! In normal times the foremast top would be visible well above the sea horizon – just another days steaming!

43. SS TALAMBA, wheelhouse & chartroom →

Combined wheelhouse and chartrooms had been around for some years at the time of this ship's construction. The long chart table complete with 'anglepoise' lamps can be seen on the left behind the radar console. The high, light coloured cabinet ran across the centre of the wheelhouse and housed telephones, light switches, the navigation light control panel, flag lockers and sundry other essentials. The auto-pilot and steering position with magnetic compass read-out above, can be seen to the right. As time progressed ships' steering wheels grew smaller and smaller, and this one would not have looked out of place in an aircraft cockpit. Although short of brasswork, the engine room telegraph still functioned in the old manner – bridge control of engines by direct lever movement had yet to appear around the fleet.

44. Engine control platform →

The main engine manoeuvring platform controls and boiler indicators are visible in this view. On the left the illuminated boiler water level indicators clearly show, whilst the main turbine controlling steam valves protrude from the right hand panel, beneath the Engineers' version of the bridge telegraph, for movements required. *Talamba* was still very much a manually operated ship, and the Duty Engineers' only respite from the intense heat was to station themselves under a large 'blower', in between dashing about the engine room on jobs. However, air conditioned control rooms were not far away. They would be brought in largely for the benefit of sophisticated electronic remote monitoring equipment!

45. Steam turbines, from above

Looking vertically down from the gratings high in the engine room, the HP and LP turbines do not look particularly impressive with their associated steam pipes. The turbine shafts powered a single propeller shaft via reduction gearing.

46. Radio Room

Sadly not the sharpest of images but this corner view of the radio room shows one desk top receiver and a transmitter on the left. The Radio Officer's regulatory 'paper' log sheets are ready for action as soon as he comes on watch for traffic lists or 'all ships' messages. The morse key was just out of shot to the right. The 'GMT' clock is clearly showing the regulatory silence periods when detection of faint distress messages might be possible. A Radio Officer's lot was a rather solitary one workwise, and receiving lengthy technical messages concerning ship's

business in times of poor reception conditions had to be something of a struggle. Apart from the maintenance of radio and navigation related equipment including aerials, the Company's Radio Officers were often able to help out with other electronic problems as such equipment multiplied around the ship.

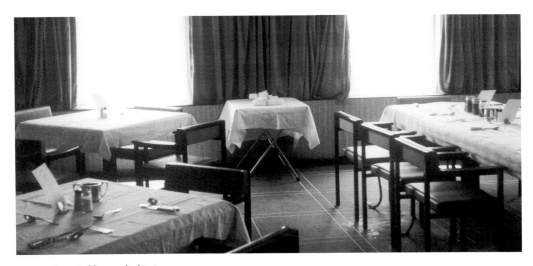

47. The Officers' dining room

The Master, all Officers and Cadets dined in this space except for the duty Engineers who could use a small mess room. In heavy weather wooden 'fiddles' could be raised around the edges of the tables to prevent cutlery, crockery and one's dinner from taking a liking to the deck. Table cloths would always be wetted to similarly slow down the escaping plates. Each chair had its own 'mooring rope' screw attachment to the deck. All of these precautions were essential and frequently needed in heavy weather swells. If nothing else, *Talamba* was a prodigious roller! At the time of the photograph, the catering crew consisted of a Chief Steward and a Chief Cook, each with their departments of staff. The Company had at the time, an extremely loyal bunch of long serving Goanese nationals around the fleet, in these capacities, an arrangement inherited from its parent P&O.

48. The Officers' wardroom

The *Talamba* by way of her unusual two funnel construction, had the benefit of a good sized swimming pool for off-duty use, situated between the funnels. The wardroom in this photograph had windows on all four sides, the forward of which had a direct door out to the pool side decking. The main access to the wardroom was from

an open style companionway up from the dining saloon just visited. A small bar in one corner tended to the Officers' off-duty refreshment needs, and proper hours were always strictly adhered to:- 1200-12.30, 1800-1900, and 2030-2200. The off duty pastimes included cards, darts and if the ship refrained from rolling too much, a version of snooker played with coloured wooden discs on a plywood faced miniature table. The latter game became surprisingly fascinating and popular to play. As with all of the Company's vessels, Anigoni's portrait of the Queen looks on from the wardroom bulkhead.

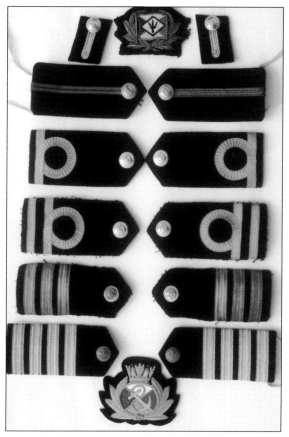

49. Company uniform insignia

Trident's identity was quickly established within the P&O Group of Companies. The trident emblem within the diamond shape readily lent itself for application to cap badges, uniform buttons, boiler suits, company stationery, and flags afloat and ashore. From the navigating officer's perspective the illustration shows from top to bottom, the complete set from Cadet to Master, through the ranks. The Trident emblem officially passed away in 1971 on the formation of P&O Bulk Shipping Division. The top badge had seen better days, and did not have a particularly good representation of the trident – appearing more like a lop-sided desert cactus in mourning black!

50. SS OTTAWA, at Gibraltar →

Such was the meteoric growth in the size of individual tankers in the 1960s that when this ship left Swan Hunter's Wallsend Yard in December 1964, she almost doubled the size of the fleet's previous largest. 100,000 ton tankers began to appear around 1960, and a few years elapsed before too many were built. *Ottawa's* vital statistics were 51,756grt and 93,231dwt on dimensions of 851ft. 10in. x 125ft. x 48ft. 02in. dr. Her cargo pumping equipment consisted of 4 x 2,000tph rated pumps, 1 x 2,000tph ballast pump and 2 x 350tph stripping pumps. Inert gas was fitted plus heating coils in the cargo tanks. A set of geared turbines produced 26,500shp at 105rpm on consumption of 132tpd, with steam produced by two Foster Wheeler ESD Boilers at 900degF, 750psi. The ship traded actively until leaner times arrived in October 1975, when she went into lay-up at Gibraltar, until February 1978. At this point Conoco bare-boat chartered the ship for off-shore storage type work in the Far East, and she went to Singapore for the conversion work required. Renamed *Udang Natuna*, the second career lasted just a little longer than her first, until she was sold in 1990. Very briefly, in 1964, this tanker had been Britain's largest! The photograph dates from 1976.

51. MV ORAMA →

Apart from the size increase, more motor ships were appearing at this time around the World's tanker fleets, giving much improved fuel economy. This ship delivered from Lithgow's, Glasgow in June 1964 becoming the Company's first motor ship. In fact the Kincaid B&W 10/84 VT2 BF180 engine briefly held the record for the largest in a British vessel. Sister ships *Opawa* and *Orissa* were similarly powered, and a speed of 16.5kts on 68tpd could be achieved. The statistics were 39,051grt, 65,972dwt on hull measurements of 775ft. x 106ft. x 43ft. 03in.dr. The ship spent ten years on time charter to Texaco before her sale in March 1974. The three ships became known as the motor 'O's, and together with the steamer *Ottawa*, had been very instrumental in the foundation days of Trident, when Texaco had needed to programme in ships to work their 'Regent' refinery, at Milford Haven. Charter arrangements would be of clear benefit to both parties.

52. SS ARDTARAIG. bridge front

British shipyards never really geared up for the construction of VLCCs in numbers, but the same could not be said of Japan. Trident placed an order for four 200,000 tonners with Mitsui of Japan, and again the individual ship size doubled. Economics at the time still favoured very large, long haul tankers with steam powered machinery. *Ardtaraig*, first of the quartet marked a major leap of faith at the time, as the big ships found full employment whilst Suez remained closed. The ship's statistics were most impressive in all directions, 119,666grt, 214,128dwt on dimensions of 1,064ft. x 157ft. 09in. x 63ft.03 in.dr. A speed of 15.6kts could be obtained on 138tpd of fuel oil from a set of geared turbines producing 28,000shp at 83rpm. The single enormous boiler, an ESD 111 Type provided steam at 61.8Kg, 513degC. A smaller auxiliary boiler of 22Kg, 220degC could power the ship in an emergency at about 7Kts. The propeller weighed 44.75 metric tonnes and measured 8.4m diameter with a 6.414m pitch. Inert gas, now a regulatory standard for all tankers, was fitted along with heating coils for all cargo tanks. Four x 3,450tph turbine driven centrifugal cargo pumps, 1 x 3,450tph ballast pump, 2 x stripping eductors, and one ballast eductor formed the pump room equipment. One area that never seemed to be standardised around the fleet was the deck paint colour scheme – this ship's being maroon. Accommodation was spacious, light and airy, and comfortably fitted out. A lift, something essential as ships grew, ran from the engine room to the bridge level with a number of intermediate stops. When new, some small-wheeled bicycles were supplied to this class of ship to speed journeys around the 1,000ft long deck. Slippery, oily decks did not ensure longevity for the bikes!

53. Bridge control of main engine →

This relatively compact wheelhouse console enabled full bridge control of the main engines. The illuminated indicator lamp is showing the status 'Bridge Control' with the tachometer at full sea speed of just over 80rpm. Such controls had to be treated with great sensitivity as serious mayhem would surely result down below, if the lever were to be yanked in the old style 'telegraph' manner. In general, the ship's Chief Engineer would be on the bridge for manouevering in port. These vessels were fully UMS (Un-manned Machinery Space) certificated, for night time operation, and quite complex setting-up procedures were followed each evening as the day workers finished, ready for night time running. A duty engineer could be automatically summoned by alarms from the engine room sounding in his cabin, or around the accommodation. Once the problem was rectified, he had to report to the bridge that the engine room was again under UMS status. Very strict procedures were always followed and logged accordingly.

54. Cargo Control Room

Another area where great changes occurred in just a few years was the way in which cargo loading, discharging and ballasting operations became remotely controlled. Tanks, pipelines, valves and gauges became not only larger, but far more spread out as the ships grew physically in size. Remote hydraulic control of valve actions became a necessity, and to dash around a VLCC taking local cargo or ballast tank ullage readings, a near impossibility even with the use of VHF two-way radios. In the photograph showing just a corner of *Ardtaraig's* cargo control room, valve and pump controls can be seen along with a couple of tank gauge dials on the right. The complex 'mimic' diagram behind was vital to operations, whether it be cargo or ballast handling underway. This space becomes the domain of the Chief Officer and Deck Officers in port, and also during tank cleaning operations at sea, the Chief Officer (or 1st Mate) is again in charge.

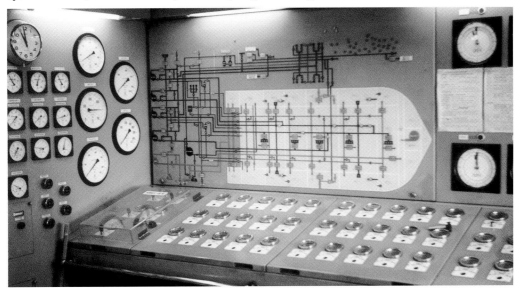

55. SS ARDSHIEL

This ship was delivered in December 1969 as the second in the quartet. In the aerial image she appears to be in part laden condition and had possibly 'lightened' at sea to a smaller tanker. This procedure was common in the 1970s, and the smaller tanker would proceed to a refinery where the larger could not hope to reach. The larger ship, now on a somewhat shallower draught, could then use a broader range of terminals than before. In 1971 *Ardshiel* played host to the journalist Noel Mostert in his preparation of a series of US magazine articles that later became the celebrated book "Supership", among the first to draw attention to the environmental problems of the big tankers.

56. SS ARDVAR →

In this photograph, *Ardvar* is in the normal ballast condition having probably unloaded somewhere at a North West European terminal. The Trident emblem can just be seen picked out on the bow, but the waviness of the black topside to boot topping paint, appears to be not up to the usual standard! The technical details of these VLCCs can be found under Nos.52 & 57.

57. In the River Tagus, Lisbon →

The magnitude of the ship's flush deck arrangement can be seen in this 1971 view taken whilst at anchor just below Lisbon. Over to the right, the giant statue of Christ faces the city from on high. *Ardvar* was the final ship of the quartet and *Ardlui* the one not illustrated. Some further statistics include – a lightship weight of 32,443 tons, a bridge to bow distance of 885ft. 10in, and bridge to stern 117ft. 02in. and height from keel to mast top 212ft. 07in., a maximum loading rate of 20,000 tph, 2 x 5 ton and 2 x 12.5 ton derricks, 3 x 20 ton anchors – this including a spare. Total cargo capacity at 98% - 252,199.7m³. Bunker capacity of 7,977m³. Fresh water 574 tons. The daily fuel consumption at sea – 143 tons. In port cargo work – 110tpd. 2 x 1,200KW IHI impulse alternators provided electrical power. The two deck cargo pipelines clearly visible in the photograph are of 800mm diameter and the normal cargo discharge rate with positive inert gas pressure was 14,000m³/hr. The ship was chartered to Chevron for ten years, and sold in 1979.

58. Helicopter rendezvous, off Cape Town

This 1971 image shows a helicopter about to hovver over the ship's designated zone for such operations. Mail, some light fresh food delivery and an occasional personnel movement might be effected in this way, some distance further out than the 'boat version' already described.

P&O Bulk Shipping "Hunt" Names	
Vessel	**Hunt**
ATHERSTONE	English fox hunt in Warwickshire and Leicestershire, centred on Atherstone and Nuneaton.
BUCCLEUCH	Scottish fox hunt (the Duke of Buccleuch's) centred on Hawick, St Boswells and Kelso in Roxburgh, Selkirk and Berwickshire (now Borders) south east Scotland.
COTSWOLD	English fox hunt in Gloucestershire around Cheltenham; after the range of hills of the same name.
DUHALLOW	Irish fox hunt in County Cork, Eire.
ERIDGE	English fox hunt on the Kent/East Sussex borders, now amalgamated into the Southdown and Eridge,
FERNIE	English fox hunt in south Leicestershire,
GRAFTON	English fox hunt in Northamptonshire and Buckinghamshire, centred on Towcester, Buckingham and Brackley,
HEYTHROP	English fox hunt in Oxfordshire and Gloucestershire around Chipping Norton, Stow-in-the-Wold and Moreton-in-Marsh,
IRFON	Welsh fox hunt (the Irfon and Towy) around Llanwrtyd Wells in Brecknock (now southern Powys,
JEDFOREST	Fox hunt in Roxburghshire (now Borders), Scotland, centred around Jedburgh and Hawick.
KILDARE	Fox hunt in County Kildare, west Wicklow, County Dublin and County Meath. Eire, centred on Dublin and Naas.
LAUDERDALE	Fox hunt in the counties of Roxburgh, Berwick, Selkirk and Midlothian in south east Scotland, centred on Melrose, Lauder, Earlston and Galashiels.
MEYNELL	English fox hunt (the Meynell and South Staffordshire) in Derbyshire, Staffordshire and Warwickshire.
NEWFOREST	English fox hunt (actually New Forest) in south west Hampshire and Wiltshire around Brockenhurst and Lyndhurst.
ORMOND	Irish fox hunt in Offaly and north Tipperary. The near repetition of the Orient Line name ORMONDE was apparently deliberate
PYTCHLEY	English Hunt in Northamptonshire. The village of Pytchley is near Kettering.
QUORN	English fox hunt in Leicestershire around Melton Mowbray, Leicester and Loughborough.
RUTLAND	(actually a tanker, rather than a bulk carrier or OBO) Pack of foxhounds (the Duke of Rutland's) hunted by the Belvoir in Leicestershire, and Lincolnshire. The hunt name is Belvoir.
SNOWDON	Welsh fox hunt (the Snowdon Valley) which hunts on foot in Snowdonia.
TAUNTON	English fox hunt In Somerset and Devon.
ULLSWATER	English fox hunt in Cumbria (Lake District).
VINE	English fox hunt (Vine and Craven) in West Berkshire.
WATERFORD	Irish fox hunt – Eire.
YORK	English fox hunt in North Yorkshire.
ZETLAND	English fox hunt in Durham.

SECTION 2. The P&O Group venture into dry bulk shipping from 1964

As the general worldwide expansion of industry and population growth continued, demand rose for the carriage of ever larger consignments of bulk commodities by sea. Coal, ores and grain for example, had been handled by hundreds of smaller traditional tramp steamers, often elderly vessels fuel hungry and requiring large crews to operate. Bulk carriers evolved, slowly at first in the 1950s, and even by 1960 there were few capable of carrying much more than 20,000 tons. The following two decades would see a near ten-fold increase in individual ship's carrying abilities. In fact, this meteoric rise fell not far short of that seen in crude oil tanker development. In 1964, the P&O Group formed a joint venture with Anglo Norness, by way of a Bermuda registered operation to market, under 'Associated Bulk Carriers', a fleet of some twenty seven vessels in the Bulk, O/B/O, and O/O categories. P&O's own first bulker entered service in 1965 with the specially merged Hain-Nourse Ltd, as managers. Unlike tankers, which tended to operate on voyage or time charters, bulk carriers operated under long term contracts of affreightment. However, just over a year later the Group's first 'OBO' went into service under Trident management, since when trading in crude oil the ships would naturally be deemed 'tankers'. Personnel on board and technical back-up ashore had of necessity to be from a tanker background, for the running of this quite sophisticated new breed of ship.

Note - as motor ships predominate henceforth, the prefix 'MV' will be dropped. A few more steamers continue to be labelled as before.

59. ATHERSTONE

Delivered to the newly merged Hain-Nourse Company in April 1965 by Hitachi of Japan, this eight hatch dry bulk carrier led the way in P&O's venture in this area of trade. *Atherstone* measured 25,992grt, 43,965dwt with dimensions of 675ft. 10in. x 90ft. 01in x 40ft. 05in.dr. Her service speed would be 15kts on 47tpd of fuel oil, plus 2tpd of diesel. To cope with fast bulk loading 3 x 750tph ballast pumps were fitted. The main engine consisted of a Hitachi, B&W 784 VT2BF, yielding some 14,700bhp at 110rpm. In the photograph the ship appears as new and the 'HN' motif can just be seen on the now dark blue funnel. It is interesting to note that Hain-Nourse started at the outset with 40,000 tonners, quite different from the 10-15,000 ton cargo ships and tramp vessels both Hain and Nourse had run for so long. Sister ships to this one were:- *Buccleuch*, *Duhallow* and *Cotswold*, described next.

60. COTSWOLD at South Shields Drydock

Many seafarers were familiar with Brigham & Cowan's repair yard at South Shields, as it featured regularly for routine dry docking and repairs. In this 1973 photograph, Hain-Nourse's *Cotswold* 25,291grt, 43,334dwt is undergoing just such work. The hull topsides appear to have an advanced case of the 'maritime measles' as they are touched up with red primer before a full coat of black topside paint. On the deck may be seen a quantity of grit sacks waiting for any blasting required on hatch covers or decks. The scene at the time was a one hundred percent normal working day on the River Tyne, but it could not be repeated today. The yard has long gone and so have the ships which kept it so busy. Beyond the *Cotswold* from left to right can be seen - a Trinity House tender moored to a buoy, an Avenue Shipping Company cargo ship, stern view of a Port Line ship in drydock, and far right behind the crane, a Gulf Oil Co. tanker. In a few days, *Cotswold* would sail in her new Bulk Shipping Division livery, for Brazil.

61. Loading at Vitoria, Brazil →

Looking resplendent in the new livery, *Cotswold* is about to be well covered in brown iron ore dust when loading at the old up-river berth opposite Vitoria City. This facility could only handle bulkers of modest dimensions, and river depths precluded sailing with a full cargo. The operation would be concluded as seen in No.62.

62. Loading at Tubarao →

Here, not many miles from Vitoria, iron ore loading is carried out on a vast scale and the largest of such carriers afloat can safely depart with a full cargo. A steady stream of the dusty brown stuff can be seen ascending the conveyor to be dropped into one of the ship's forward holds. Just three hatches remain open for completion before sailing.

MV COTSWOLD Bulk Carrier

Summer Deadweight	43,334 long tons	Grt	25,291
Total Hold Capacity	1,821,789 cu.ft.	Loa	675ft
Summer Laden Draught	40ft 05in	Br	90ft

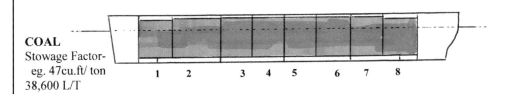

COAL
Stowage Factor-
   eg. 47cu.ft/ ton
38,600 L/T

A voyage from Norfolk, Virginia to Kawasaki, Japan via the Panama Canal

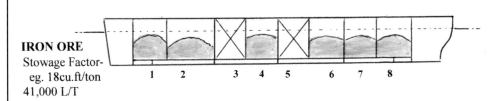

IRON ORE
Stowage Factor-
   eg. 18cu.ft/ton
41,000 L/T

A voyage from Vitoria and Tubarao in Brazil, to Emden, Germany

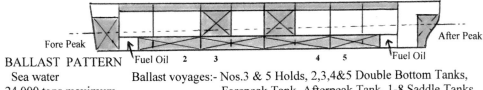

Fore Peak   After Peak
Fuel Oil   2   3   4   5   Fuel Oil

BALLAST PATTERN
   Sea water   Ballast voyages:- Nos.3 & 5 Holds, 2,3,4&5 Double Bottom Tanks,
24,000 tons maximum   Forepeak Tank, Afterpeak Tank, 1-8 Saddle Tanks
ie. 55% of deadweight

Notes-
Stowage Factors for dry bulk cargoes vary considerably Worldwide
with differing grades of cargo from the many mines and quarries.
'Angles of Repose' are dependent on particle/lump size and moisture
content of the commodity involved.

Example- Natural angle of repose at stockpile 'cone'. 45 degrees

(Drawing No.5 COTSWOLD Cargo Stowage plan)

63. ERIDGE

At this point it will perhaps be helpful to note that a few ships may now seem out of proper Company order, and context. Although the OBOs were initially placed under Trident Tankers' wing, as later developments show, they would become grouped with the dry bulkers just five years later, when the two fleets merged. *Eridge* delivered in October 1966 from Mitsui, Japan and measured 42,825grt and 72,692dwt on 823ft. x 104ft. x 45ft.dr. These dimensions were generally termed 'Panamax' implying passage possible through that waterway. A Mitsui-B&W engine type 984-VT2 8F180 could propel the ship at a laden speed of 15kts on 68tpd of fuel oil plus 2tpd diesel, providing 17,600bhp at 108rpm. Oil cargo equipment included 2 x 2,500tph Drysdale cargo pumps along with 2 x 320tph stripping pumps. Ballast operations were handled by 2 x 1,200tph pumps. An inert gas plant was fitted in accordance with tanker regulations. A pair of traditional tanker style hose handling derricks were installed at the shore connection manifolds.

CERTIFICATE OF INCORPORATION

ON CHANGE OF NAME

No. 258949 /117

I hereby certify that

ASIATIC STEAM NAVIGATION COMPANY LIMITED

having by special resolution and with the approval of the Secretary of State changed its name, is now incorporated under the name of

P & O BULK SHIPPING LIMITED

Given under my hand at Cardiff he 4TH JULY 1977

D.A. Pendlebury
D. A. PENDLEBURY

Assistant Registrar of Companies

64. FERNIE

Few ships could claim to be something other than what was intended, but this proved to be one of them! Completed as a straight bulk carrier, the nine hatch *Fernie* was the end result of an order placed for four OBOs:- three in Japan, and one with the Fairfield Shipyard as a "sop" to the then struggling British Shipbuilding industry. The yard 'collapsed' and although the order was replaced in Japan, it was for a straight bulk carrier, not an OBO. This ship entered the dry bulk service in June 1967, and her measurements were - 36,908grt, 74,422dwt on 825ft x 107ft 04in x 44ft. 08in. dr. On 65tpd plus 2tpd diesel, she could achieve 15.25kts service speed. To cope with fast loadings, 3 x 1,000tph ballast pumps were fitted. The main engine type was the same as No.63, but could produce 18,900bhp at 110rpm. She was sold on in 1978. In the photograph the large 'HN' monogram is visible on the funnel.

65. GRAFTON →

Side sliding hatch cover trackways, much additional deck piping and the two derrick posts readily distinguish the OBO from the bulker. This was ship delivered from the Japanese, Hitachi yard in April 1967, and would trade alternately between oil and ore cargoes during her eleven year stint with Trident / P&O Bulk Shipping. Technically this ship differed little from No.63. Unsurprisingly, these vessels were somewhat complex to operate, and strict 'changeover' procedures had to be followed when changing from oil to bulk, and vice versa. Apart from large tank cleaning machines, which stowed beneath the hatch covers when not required, 'liftagrid' cargo heating coils had to be lowered, or raised accordingly in the holds.

66. Launch of HEYTHROP →

In June 1967 Hitachi of Japan launched the third and final OBO of the series for Trident. The photograph from the time of the launch shows a typical colourful Japanese traditional ceremony with bunting, balloons and flags. This ship's tonnages were 43,330grt and 73,800dwt with a 'light ship' weight of 17,652 tons. Technically much the same as Nos 63 & 65, apart from the oil cargo classification, these vessels had the notation 'Bulk Carrier strengthened for ore cargoes'. In 1978 *Heythrop* went to Greek owners and continued to trade until scrapping in 1983.

67. HEYTHROP at Priolo, Sicily →

The ship's first regular employment involved a cross Mediterranean time charter carrying crude oil from North Africa to Sicily. In the 1968 photograph and still looking 'as new' the vessel is in her regular berth in the corner of Augusta Harbour, Sicily unloading via one shore boom. Anchored ahead in the distance is one of the then few remaining WW2 T2 tankers still in service – *Conoco Humber*.

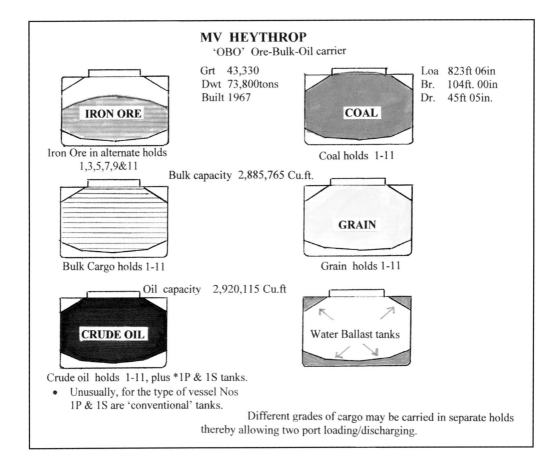

MV HEYTHROP
'OBO' Ore-Bulk-Oil carrier

Grt   43,330
Dwt 73,800tons
Built 1967

Loa 823ft 06in
Br.   104ft. 00in
Dr.   45ft 05in.

IRON ORE

COAL

Iron Ore in alternate holds
1,3,5,7,9&11

Coal holds 1-11

Bulk capacity 2,885,765 Cu.ft.

GRAIN

Bulk Cargo holds 1-11

Grain holds 1-11

Oil capacity   2,920,115 Cu.ft

CRUDE OIL

Water Ballast tanks

Crude oil holds 1-11, plus *1P & 1S tanks.
- Unusually, for the type of vessel Nos 1P & 1S are 'conventional' tanks.

Different grades of cargo may be carried in separate holds thereby allowing two port loading/discharging.

68. In Drydock, Marseilles →

The first dry docking after construction of a merchant ship is generally referred to as the 'guarantee docking', since the opportunity may be taken to rectify anything found not to be up to specification, during the first year's service. Here in Marseilles, with the ship just a year old in 1968, the anchor cables have been ranged for shackle re-marking in the traditional way. Owing to the use of sea-berth type loading terminals, the Charterer had requested more shackles (12) be on the starboard cable, as opposed to just (10) on the port side. It is customary for equal scopes of chain to be on both anchors. This ship's anchors weighed 188cwt, or 9.4 tons apiece.

← 69.   One of the largest
        'Trident' funnel marks.

Black topside paint has inevitably strayed in the
breeze on to the stone coloured bulwark which
will need touching up. This Trident funnel logo
was particularly distinctive, and could be seen
for miles around, in port or at sea.

70. Attention to the propeller

This dry dock photograph conveys scale better
than most, since the draught marks have just
been picked out freshly in white against the new
red anti-fouling paint. Work is continuing on
checking and re-securing the propeller and boss,
various engine room sea valve boxes and grills.
The giant propeller boss key can be seen down
by the blocks upon which the ship sits.

CERTIFICATE OF INCORPORATION
ON CHANGE OF NAME

No. 80868 / 153

I hereby certify that

TRIDENT TANKERS LIMITED

having by special resolution and with the approval of the Secretary of State changed
its name, is now incorporated under the name of

LAURITZEN PENINSULAR REEFERS (U.K.) LIMITED

Given under my hand at London the 18TH OCTOBER 1973

N Taylor.
(N. TAYLOR)

Assistant Registrar of Companies

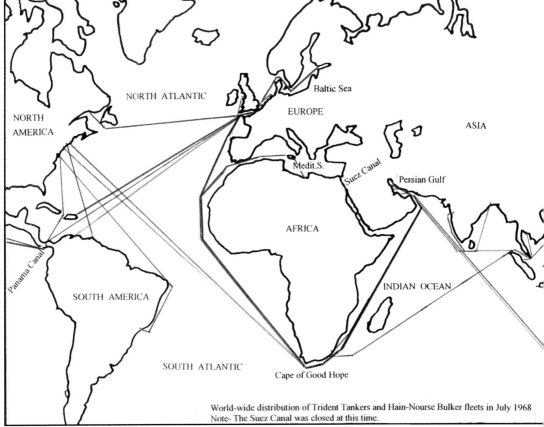

World-wide distribution of Trident Tankers and Hain-Nourse Bulker fleets in July 1968
Note- The Suez Canal was closed at this time.

← 71. HEYTHROP, Cargo Control Room

Vertical column tank level remote reading gauges are on the left of this corner view of the control room. Some of the hydraulic valve control levers are on the right. When this new type of ship entered service there were serious fears about stability problems arising from the anticipated 'free-surface' effect in the vast oil cargo holds, especially as the ships loaded or discharged. If a serious list developed for any reason the ship's ability to remain upright might be impaired. Particularly sophisticated valve systems were installed with 'interlocks' which prohibited the opening of more than just a couple of hold valves at the same time. As experience in service grew, the problem did not cause major worries, however particular care was always exercised to keep this class of ship as bolt upright as possible.

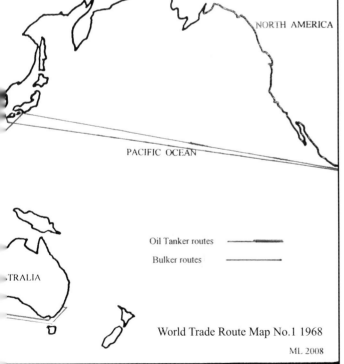

NORTH AMERICA

PACIFIC OCEAN

Oil Tanker routes   —————

Bulker routes   —————

.TRALIA

World Trade Route Map No.1 1968

ML 2008

72. Bridge control of main engine.

This pedestal housed the ship's direct 'bridge to main engine controls'. Photographed in port at 'F.W.E.', the nearby tachometer is naturally, stationary. At sea, or for manouevering some 17,600bhp were available at one's finger tips. For the engine type see No. 63. Before moving on to the next ship, a brief summary of a very serious incident in the life of this vessel follows. In November 1971 whilst rounding the South African coast, an explosion occurred in No.11 hold, fortunately without injury to personnel. Fire spread to, and gutted the greater part of the accommodation block and the ship had to be abandoned. Duly reboarded, she was taken into Port Elizabeth for damage assessment and later, fully repaired, went back into trade.

73. SS IRFON, fitting out at Kiel

This photograph appears courtesy of ©P&O Heritage Collection (DP World). Seen here in 1971, the ship is in the latter stages of fitting out alongside after the launch. She entered service in November that year and was the first of three larger OBOs to come into service. Ships of this type effectively doubled in size in about five years, and this one's tonnages were- 82,206grt and 150,000dwt. Perhaps, even with hindsight, it is somewhat surprising that the vessel's chosen power plant was steam turbine. The subsequent OBOs were all motor ships. *Irfon's* dimensions were 946ft. 09in x 142ft. 05in x 57ft. 05in.dr. A speed of 14.7kts laden could be achieved on 128tpd, plus 3tpd diesel. The main engine consisted of a set of A.E.G turbines producing 24,000shp, steam being supplied by 2 x Babcock & Wilcox Marine Radiant boilers at 960degF, 880psi. When operating in the crude oil trade, 2 x 4,500tph cargo pumps handled the discharge, with one 300tph stripping pump. Ballast operations were conducted by 2 x 1,500tph pumps. The ship had a rather erratic career – she went into lay-up at Venice from April 1975 to February 1979; then re-entered trade until February 1980. Next she went into Far East off-shore oil storage employment from March 1980 until sold in July 1985. The motor propelled 150,000 tonners had no such interruption to their careers – their fuel consumption being in the order of 20-25 tpd less. Simple economics prevailed.

74. JEDFOREST →

Of very similar dimensions to No.73; 956ft. 10in, x 148ft. 02in. x 55ft.09in.dr., this vessel's tonnages were 83,714grt and 152,461dwt. Swedish built by Eriksberg, she was delivered to the Company in May 1972. At the time of her construction yard space was at a premium due to full order books. Eriksbergs at Gothenburg hit upon a novel solution to the dilemma by subcontracting part construction of the hull to Lisnave of Portugal. The forepart, from bow to No.6 hold, was duly built and towed up-Channel to be welded to the more complex after part. This unusual assembly system worked well as *Jedforest* proved to be a good, steady performer in service. The two-part construction technique enabled Eriksbergs to speedily produce a number of large bulkers, OBOs and →

SECTION 3. The P&O Bulk Shipping Division era, 1971-1980

During 1971 there were major reorganisations within the P&O Group generally. These resulted from the 1970 deliberations of management consultants McKinsey and Company. The far ranging recommendations would lead to the consolidation of many individual Group companies into just a handful of major divisions for the future. Trident Tankers and Hain-Nourse would logically be merged into the single entity of P&O Bulk Shipping Division. This new management and operational structure then took over all aspects of running the tankers, bulkers and gas ships. Responsibility would also later lie within this Division for involvement in the several part-owned and associate companies; eg.- Associated Bulk Carriers, Bulk Shipping Associates, LNG Carriers and Panocean-Anco. The next few years would see expansion in the gas trade, a larger series of OBOs, but only two new product tankers entering service. The older tankers were disposed of one by one without replacement, and most had gone by 1980. New gas tankers continued to be added to the fleet until 1979.

A note is necessary here concerning General Cargo Division to aid explanation of later events. This division would see the merger of the Group's many general cargo ship owning subsidiaries into a single unit in 1971. Whilst this particular restructuring was vital as fleets became decimated by the ever advancing containerisation of their traditional services, it nevertheless saw the demise of some historically significant companies such as – British India Steam Navigation Co. Ltd and New Zealand Shipping Co. Ltd. Yet, as late as 1973, there were still some seventy five general cargo and refrigerated cargo ships operating, along with seven containerships managed for OCL. Such vessel types remaining will be described in Section 4.

tankers in the early 1970s. Power was provided by an EMV B&W 8K 98FF motor, with an output of 28,000bhp at 103rpm on a daily consumption of 105tpd fuel oil, and 5tpd diesel. Oil cargoes were handled by 4 x 2,500tph pumps plus 2 x 300tph stripping pumps. For ballast operations 2 x 2,000tph pumps were fitted. All pumps, deck machinery including winches and windlasses and heating coils for the oil cargoes, were steam supplied by 2 x Blohm & Voss boilers. The ship had a good length active career, and would not be sold until February 1987. In the photograph she appears to have just unloaded a particularly dusty bulk cargo. This may have been after a rare bulk tapioca run from Thailand to Europe. The sickly smell of bulk tapioca could be detected around the ship for months afterwards. The cargo was believed to have gone for animal feed. From this image onwards, the ship's funnel markings consist of the new P&O bright blue background, plus the 'shadow' P&O logo in white.

75. Coal discharge, Muroran, Japan

Back into the more regular coal trade, here in 1981 the ship is unloading a part cargo of coal in Japan's North Island. Three giant grab conveyors are making short work of the remaining cargo, the rest having departed in Kimitsu. Despite a major imminent job to clean the hatch tops and decks, coal was not regarded as a particularly bad cargo – it tended to polish the hold steelwork. This particular cargo had been loaded in Norfolk, Virginia.

76. Coal loading, Hay Point, Australia

A couple of weeks later and the reverse operation was underway in Queensland; this cargo's destination – the Mediterranean area. A large telescopic loader is pouring the fine black stuff into a hold. The device is designed to prevent coal breakage and dust, but since it was the height of the rainy season, the stockpiles were anything but dusty!

77. JEDFOREST, Southern Indian Ocean sunset

For an interesting weather comparison – look back to No.42! On sailing from Queensland, a long heavy swell was encountered from the South Australian coast almost to South Africa. The only external sign of life spotted –wandering albatross –always seemed to know when galley scraps were due to go overboard! When this photograph was taken the ocean swell had finally dropped away, and a mail call at Cape Town anticipated soon. Long trips of this nature, given dry conditions on deck could be highly beneficial for maintenance and painting – all eleven hatch tops were prepared and re-coated.

78. KILDARE

The technical description for the last vessel holds good as this ship was an identical sister vessel albeit not built in two halves. In the aerial photograph the 'P&O logo' clearly shows on the funnel and another break with tradition has been made – the stone coloured upper works have turned white. *Kildare* delivered from Eriksberg in October 1972 and traded for Bulk Shipping until sold on in February 1987 however, she was 'chartered back' until 1988. This became a more common practice in latter years.

79. NEWFOREST

Originally operating under the name *Koll*, thereafter *Lake Tahoe*, this OBO joined the bulk fleet in October 1983 to trade as a dry bulker, having initially been on time charter. Very similar to the previous two ships described, she remained in the fleet only until May 1985.

80. SS LAUDERDALE

Steam power and its greater fuel consumption could still compete as late as 1972 when installed in very large ships making long haul runs. This Ore/Oil carrier was indeed a 'one off' for P&O Bulk, and she would remain in a class of her own. Handed over to the Company in December 1972 by Mitsubishi of Japan, she automatically took the top position regarding size. Tonnages were 143,959grt and 260,412dwt on dimensions of 1,099ft (335m) x 175ft 10in.(53.6m) x 67ft.07in.(20.61m. dr.). The engine consisted of a set of Mitsubishi steam turbines generating some 32,000shp at 90rpm taking steam from 2 x MHI CEV2M-8N boilers at 61.2Kg, 515degC. Daily consumption amounted to 160tpd, at 15kts laden speed. For cargo pumping 2 x 6,000tph turbine powered centrifugal pumps, plus a 450tph stripping pump were fitted, along with a 3,000tph ballast pump. Although earlier described under 'ship types', it is evident from the photograph just how narrow the central iron ore hatches and holds were in this class of vessel. The large wing tanks are similar to conventional tanker construction. Crude oil was carried in all central hold and wing tanks to reach the full deadweight of cargo. Iron ore, being very dense would only be loaded in the central holds to achieve the same aim. After ten years of very successful trading the ship was sold in May 1982 for further trading.

81. MEYNELL →

Another product of Mitsubishi, this bulk carrier delivered to the Company at the end of 1973. At 69,110grt, 127,346dwt her dimensions were 856ft. 03in. x 133ft. x 57ft. 09in.dr. An MHI Sulzer 8RND90 engine developing 20,880bhp at 118rpm gave a speed of 15kts laden on 82tpd, plus 3tpd diesel. Ballast operations were handled by 3 x 1,500tph pumps. She served the Company until sold in December 1983.

82. AURORA →

Managed on behalf of Bulk Shipping Associates Ltd, in which P&O had a 25% interest, this 79,620grt, 152,050dwt bulk carrier came from Sunderland Shipbuilders Ltd, in November 1975. In February 1986 she became fully owned by the Company, was sold on with a charter back, and finally left the fleet during 1987. A Harland & Wolf B&W engine produced 28,000bhp at 103rpm. Two Aalborg Verft auxiliary boilers provided steam for services. In the photograph the ship has evidently just discharged a coal cargo somewhere in NW Europe, judging by the hatch top dust. Coal and iron ore remain the most regular of cargoes for this class of vessel, today.

83. ARDMAY

In 1974 the Company ordered two motor product tankers from Horten Shipyard in Norway, a specialist in such types at the time. *Ardmay* and sister ship *Ardmore* were designed for worldwide clean oil trading on either the 'spot' market or long term charters. This first ship 19,144grt, 31,600dwt delivered in June 1975, and makes an interesting comparison to No.31 of 1962. The new ships could carry some 30,000 tons of cargo against just 20,000 for the earlier vessels, yet consumed only 38tpd instead of 53tpd. Undoubtedly more efficient, the extra cargo could be carried by way of a 15ft.increase in beam, and 5ft. greater draught – the overall length being 6ft. shorter. The two ships' dimensions were 553ft. 08in. x 85ft. x 36ft.07in.dr. A Horten Sulzer 6RND76 of 12,000bhp gave 15.3kts laden. The propeller was a 'keyless' manganese bronze type weighing 17,170Kg and 5.9m in diameter. Two Sunrod boilers provided steam to 4 x Worthington Simpson cargo pumps which had an integral 'vac-strip' tank drainage system each. A Howden inert gas generator produced 4,000m³/hr to the cargo tanks. The anchors, port, starboard and spare, each weighed 6,900KG, and eleven shackles of cable were fitted port and starboard. 2 x 10 ton derricks handled the cargo hoses and a 3 ton stores gantry crane worked across the after deck. The total crew complement averaged around 38 persons.

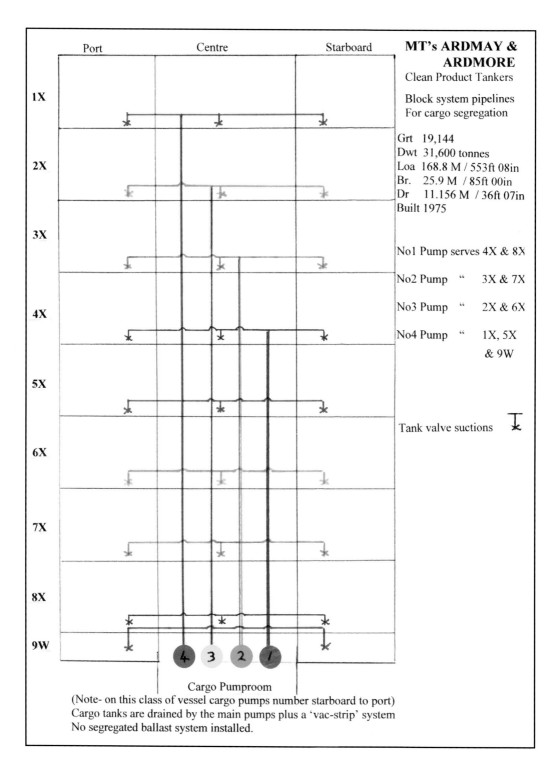

MT's ARDMAY & ARDMORE

Clean Product Tankers

Block system pipelines
For cargo segregation

Grt 19,144
Dwt 31,600 tonnes
Loa 168.8 M / 553ft 08in
Br. 25.9 M / 85ft 00in
Dr 11.156 M / 36ft 07in
Built 1975

No1 Pump serves 4X & 8X

No2 Pump " 3X & 7X

No3 Pump " 2X & 6X

No4 Pump " 1X, 5X
              & 9W

Tank valve suctions

Port   Centre   Starboard

1X
2X
3X
4X
5X
6X
7X
8X
9W

Cargo Pumproom

(Note- on this class of vessel cargo pumps number starboard to port)
Cargo tanks are drained by the main pumps plus a 'vac-strip' system
No segregated ballast system installed.

84. In Long Island Sound, U.S.A.

The scene is winter 1977 as *Ardmay* pushes through thin ice in Long Island Sound – the temperature was -10deg.C – a great change from the voyage start in the Caribbean, just a few days earlier. Although a considerable advance on the earlier steam tankers described, in most respects this ship was quite conventional. Traditional hose handling derricks have yet to be replaced by the hydraulic deck cranes of the 1980s, and beyond.

85. Hudson River, New York State

On this inland voyage leg the ship is taking a part cargo of clean petroleum products the 140 miles up-river to Albany, the State Capital. This is the limit for sea-going craft and a part cargo had already been off-loaded at a New York anchorage to barges attended by pusher-tugs. With the city quickly lost astern, the wooded hills and banks of the Hudson make a sudden contrast to the bustle of New York. *Ardmay* was sold for further trading in April 1983.

86. ARDMORE →

Sister ship to No.85, this one delivered from the builders in Norway just a few months later. In all respects similar to *Ardmay*, her career under P&O Bulk Shipping Division lasted until June 1983. Panocean, in which P&O had a 50% interest, not elaborated upon in this book, also had some tankers of similar design built at the Horten Shipyard, but they were of the more sophisticated and specialist chemical cargo type.

Note- A review of the liquefied gas carrier fleet follows.

87. GAZANA →

Ordered towards the end of the Trident era, and actually launched with the 'Trident' funnel logo, this ship's entry into service was much delayed until February 1972. Serious problems at the Cammell Laird Shipyard on Merseyside would finally see this ship and sister *Gambada*, come into service under Bulk Shipping Division control, with the new blue 'P&O' funnel. In fact the Group entry into the gas tanker trade, a logical progression from oil tankers, did not seem to be a high profile affair at all. Yet the embryonic fleet would soon expand and trade around the World very successfully. In the photograph the ship appears to be in ex drydocking condition, complete with the 'un-official' P&O flag painted on the bridge front. This became popular on a number of Company ships. *Gazana's* statistics were 21,357grt and 21,684dwt, however in the gas trades ships are normally described in terms of their cargo volume capacity - ie in this case 29,791m³. Dimensions were 177.78m x 26.0m x 9.86m.dr. The main engine type was a Kincaid built B&W 8K74EF rated at 13,720bhp on 120rpm. A laden speed of 16.0kts and ballast of 17.0kts could be achieved on a consumption of 51tpd, and 4tpd of diesel. A Spanner auxiliary boiler was fitted together with an inert gas generator for cargo operations. The cargo pumps, one 'Deepwell' type for each cargo tank, consisted of 8 x 316m³/hr units. The electric motors for the pumps reside on the tank dome top, and extended vertical drive shafts pass down through the tanks to the pump wells below. By the very nature of LPG cargo, sophisticated central control systems exist for loading, discharging, monitoring of pressures and levels, changes of cargo grade and gas freeing. Compressors take 'boil-off' cargo vapour continuously to re-liquefy and return it to the tanks. The refrigerated gas tankers' main cargoes are Butane, Propane and Ammonia carried at -0.5degC, -43degC and -33degC respectively at just a fraction above atmospheric pressure. Cargo tanks are constructed out of special low temperature grade steel. In 1980 these two ships underwent a major conversion to enable carriage of Vinyl Chloride Monomer and Propylene Oxide for a time charter. *Gazana* was sold in the 1986 gas fleet demise, becoming *Havjarl*.

88. GAMBADA

In all respects the same as No.87, this ship eventually delivered from Cammell Laird in March 1973, well into the Bulk Shipping Division era. In the photograph she is manouevering away from a berth a few miles below Baton Rouge, Louisiana at the start of a new trade, carrying the special products just described above, to the Far East. The cluttered decks of refrigerated gas tankers make something of a contrast to to those of the oil tankers, nevertheless space has been found for a traditional pair of midships hose handling derricks. Stores cranes spanned the after deck. *Gambada* also left the fleet in 1986 becoming *Hesiod*.

89. GAMBADA at Freeport, Texas →

Seen arriving from her Genoa Drydock conversion job, the ship is about to take on liquid nitrogen in readiness for the loading of two tanks with Propylene Oxide. Clearly visible is the cargo control room perched on high atop the compressor room, the two high mast riser vents, and a forward pair of deck pressure vessels (DPVs). These form ambient storage for product likely to be carried next. Sufficient liquid kept in a DPV would then be used to 'gas-up' and cool down the main tanks in readiness for loading.

90. Cargo Control Room →

There are far fewer valves, tanks and pipelines on a gas tanker than an oil tanker, but the degree of complexity required to carry sub zero liquid cargo is much greater. Pump controls, tank level gauges, pressure readouts, monitoring of re-liquefaction, compressor operation, heat exchangers, booster pumps and normal ballast procedures are all covered. Additionally, atmospheric gas monitoring remotely of numerous spaces around the cargo area must be continuously maintained for the ship's safe operation.

91. Loading on the River Mississippi

With the courtesy US flag flying from the starboard yard arm, *Gambada* is seen here in this 1980 photograph well advanced in the loading of Vinyl Chloride Monomer (VCM). Although of special low temperature suitability, the 'chiksan' loading arm is of a design familiar all around the World's terminals.

92. GAMBADA, deck equipment →

The view down from the bridge top shows the mightily cluttered deck full of essential equipment. Each pair of low temperature cargo tanks share a 'dome' structure which passes through the ship's actual steel deck construction. In this image the top of No.3 P&S tank dome is where the green canvas covered electric motors can be seen. The pipework, gauging, safety valves and access points are situated adjacent. A pair of additional white 'framed' small pressure vessels, have been added to sustain a blanket of nitrogen over the two tanks converted for the carriage of the Propylene Oxide. This was done by way of the 'framed' nitrogen vapouriser unit alongside the white tanks. The smaller LPG ships were certainly not so handy for on deck maintenance work!

93. GARMULA →

Delivered in July 1972 from the Moss Rosenberg Shipyard, this 52,648m^3 capacity gas tanker measured 32,213grt and just 38,820dwt. For the size of ship involved, gas tanker deadweights always seem small, and this is simply due to the very low gravity of the liquid refrigerated gas. By no means a small ship, this one's physical dimensions were 207.1m x 31.4m x 11.3m dr. A Sulzer 7RND90 engine provided 18,270bhp on 118rpm for a speed of 16.5kts laden. An inert gas generator and an Aalborg oil/exhaust gas boiler for service requirements were fitted. Eight x 370m^3/hr cargo pumps handled the discharge. The ship's two DPVs can be seen painted white. In 1979 the ship passed to Mundogas ownership (in which P&O had a minority interest between 1970 and 1984) and was renamed *Mundogas America*. She remained managed by P&O until 1984.

94. GAMBHIRA

Unusually, this little ship was a second hand purchase in 1973 for specific charter requirements. She had been launched by Astilleros, Cadiz in 1969 as *Butaneuve*. At 13,800m³, her tonnages were 11,544grt and 11,460dwt. A Manises Sulzer 6RD-76 provided 9,600bhp at 119rpm on 35tpd fuel oil. A stern anchor was fitted. Cargo pumps included 4 x 142m³/hr and 4 x 250m³/hr. Her new name following the 1986 clear-out, was *Havpil*.

95. SS LNG CHALLENGER ↗

The photograph is seen courtesy of ©P&O Heritage Collection (DP World)

When completed in October 1974 by Moss Rosenberg, Stavanger, this ship seemed to be a giant leap of faith for P&O. She would come to be owned by LNG Carriers Ltd, a consortium of P&O, Fearnley & Eger, and A.P.Moller. The ship proved essentially to be some years ahead of her time as the long distance LNG trade did not expand to any degree for years to come. Sadly, *LNG Challenger* and one or two other owners' similar vessels, such as Ocean's *Nestor*, would spend many of their early years in lay-up. This ship had such spells in Bahrein, Augusta, Lisbon and Vestnes, Norway. Finally in 1979 she entered a regular trade from North Africa to the East Coast of the U.S.A. under the abbreviated name of *Pollenger*. The change was reportedly so as not to draw environmentalists' attention to what she was carrying! In October 1985 LNG Carriers became fully P&O owned. Sold after a two year lay-up in a Norweigian fjord in 1979, she went to Far Eastern owners in Japan as *Asake Maru*. Eventually long awaited LNG contracts did appear as gas projects came on stream, and today this ship is still actively trading under her 6th name as *Margaret Hill*, (2008). Her time did eventually come! Turning to the ship's technical data, there were just five giant cargo tanks subdivided port and starboard, and built of special low temperature alloy material. Special surrounding insulation material had to withstand the effects of methane cargo carried at -161degC. The 'boil-off' from the cargo on this type of vessel can be fed to the boilers as fuel on passage. Methane's density is 0.425. In the photograph the ship may well have been undergoing her first 'gassing-up' trials. The distinctive funnel marking was that of LNG Carriers Ltd, and the giant stern loading gantry believed to have been installed for a Far East project, was never used in earnest. In recent years it was removed completely. The ship's tonnage measurements were 72,357grt, 52,050dwt with a cargo capacity of 87,600m³. Dimensions were 249.5m x 40m x 10.5m dr. – equating to a large vessel yet a small deadweight, given that ultra light cargo density of Methane. Cargo handling was by 10 x 750m³/hr pumps and ballast operations by 2 x 1,200m³/hr pumps. The main engine consisted of General Electric steam turbines delivering some 30,000shp at 95rpm. Two Foster Wheeler ESD3 boilers of 63.3KG/cm² and 513degC provided the steam. Today there are numerous giant LNG ships trading in several areas of the world, especially in the Middle and Far East.

96. GARBETA

Another product of the Moss Rosenberg Shipyard, this LPG carrier entered service in October 1975. Of 16,200grt and 22,561m³, she served the Company until 1986 when sold and the name *Hermod* applied. Two notable changes can be seen in the image – the traditional midships derricks have gone in favour of a long reach hydraulic crane, and two totally enclosed lifeboats are becoming the 'norm'. *Garbeta's* statistics were 165m x 23.3m x 10.3m.dr.

97. GANDARA

Of similar proportions to No.96, this ship was built by Swan Hunter and delivered in April 1976. Her cubic capacity amounted to 22,711m³ and the profile differed since three DPVs were installed, and the compressor room/ cargo control room was sited further aft. Another feature then becoming more common was the flush deck arrangement from forward to aft, whereby no raised forecastle or poop deck existed. This ship remained until the 1986 sale and then took the name *Helikon*.

98. GARINDA

First of a quartet of larger LPG carriers to be built by Thyssen at Emden, Germany for the Company in what proved to be something of a financial stretch. This programme of new building turned out to be the last as such regarding gas ships, as they were paid for in Deutschemarks whose value against the pound was steadily rising. *Garinda* entered service in March 1977 and at 34,895grt with a capacity of 54,226m³, she represented a major size increase compared to the majority of the LPG fleet. Dimensions were-219.5m x 28.55m x 11.48m.dr. The main engine type was a MAN K6 SZ90/160A rated at 19,920bhp on 122rpm. Eight x 400m³/hr cargo pumps handled the discharges and 2 x 480m³/hr pumps worked the ballast system. This class of vessel was generally referred to as the 'Rheinstahls'. All went in the 1986 clear-out to Mhyre Havtor but continued to be P&O managed until 1987. This ship became *Hekabe*.

World-wide distribution of P&O Bulk Shipping ves

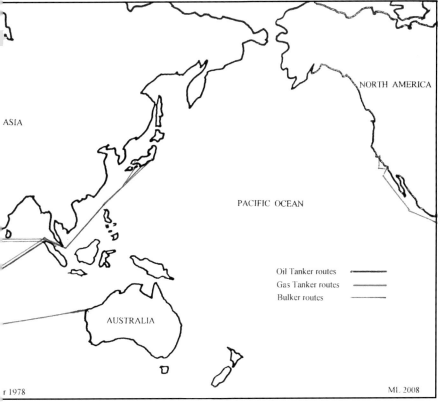

99. GARALA

The ship is seen here at full tilt through the Dover Strait by which time an all red deck and white superstructure livery, appears to prevail around the fleet. The four vessels were technically the same, and in the final fleet demise, the 1979 built *Garala* became *Hemina*, *Galconda* became *Havkong*, and *Galpara's* new name was *Havdrott*.

ASIA

NORTH AMERICA

PACIFIC OCEAN

Oil Tanker routes

Gas Tanker routes

Bulker routes

AUSTRALIA

r 1978

ML 2008

SECTION 4. The P&O Deep Sea Cargo Division era 1981-1984

By 1981 there had been a great reduction in ship numbers in both the General Cargo Division and the Bulk Shipping Division. In the face of increasing operating costs and ever present competition from the Far East, it was inevitable that further consolidation and rationalisation would be on the agenda. Deep Sea Cargo Division would draw the remaining elements of its two predecessors together, in the search for operational economy. Such would be the reduction in actively trading ship numbers, and therefore sea staff and shore staff alike, that the period would best be remembered for disposals only. By the Spring of 1983 just a handful of tankers, bulkers and OBOs, plus the gas ships remained from BSD. A mere five reefers and just three cargo ships survived from the GCD side and the latter were being managed for OCL. There were still a number of associate companies wherein the Company maintained some financial interest. One new positive development arising from the 'shrinkage' would see the utilisation of both sea staff and shore staff in the management of other owners' ships. This development is partly covered here, but mainly in the following section.

100. DWARKA

The photograph is seen courtesy of ©P&O Heritage Collection. (DP World) Appearing as if from another age, and indeed she was, is the classic little passenger/ cargo liner *Dwarka*. Of just 4,867grt she had originally been one of a quartet of British India ships engaged in the migrant labour and cargo trade between Bombay, Karachi and the Gulf ports. Delivered in December 1947 by Swan Hunter & Wigham Richardson, she retained her distinctive livery throughout thirty seven years on the same run. The ship's vital statistics were 398ft 07in x 54ft. 09in x 21ft. 11in.dr. A Doxford 2SA, 5 cylinder oil engine provided 13.5knots, whilst other services were supplied by two donkey boilers. There were two decks with a third in the area of No.1 hold, and the accommodation originally allowed for - thirteen 1st Class Passengers, forty one 2nd class, and nine hundred un-berthed. Lounges and dining rooms were air conditioned. The ship's name had been used before on a B.I. East Africa service vessel from 1922. Sister ship names were:- *Dara, Daressa & Dumra*. By the 1970s passenger numbers on the route had been steadily eroded away by the airlines, therefore in 1982 under Deep Sea Cargo Division control, *Dwarka's* long career finally terminated. In the photograph, date unknown, a good crowd appear to be onboard, but judging by the draught, not much cargo. The reason for the celebratory flags is unclear, but the ship does have two modern radar scanners fitted, indicating a late date in her long service. This vessel must have been about the last to 'get away with' the old fashioned nested lifeboat stowage.

102. VENDEE →

Another Swan Hunter built vessel, this one entered service in January 1972 as British India's *Zaida* 6,406grt, 8,365dwt on the New Zealand / Japan service. Along with sister ship *Vosges*, ex. *Zira*, the design permitted handling of palletised fruit and refrigerated cargo, by way of ship side access doors for fork lift trucks, in addition to hatches above. Seen in the photograph in later years with a single deck crane, she was running to the UK from the Eastern Mediterranean. Both ships received their second name in 1975, and served right through to P&O Ship Management days, being sold in 1986

101.   STRATHMAY

This attractively designed ship emerged from Swan Hunter's yard in September 1970 as British India's *Manora*. The three others in the class were – *Merkara*, *Morvada* and *Mulbera* and in the 1975 re-branding of P&O's general cargo fleet the names became – *Strathmeigle*, *Strathmore*, and *Strathmuir* respectively. The latter when sold, would remain briefly under P&O Management in 1983-4 as *Sonia M*. The unstoppable spread of containerisation is in evidence in this photograph, albeit with just a few boxes lashed on hatch tops. The 'M' class cargo liners were deemed quite advanced in their day with deck cranes, twin hatches and heavy lift capability. Tonnages were 11,208grt and 13,300dwt. The other three ships were under P&O Deep Sea Cargo Division control from 1981-1982.

103. WILD CURLEW

In 1971 P&Os Federal Steam Navigation Company and the old established Danish firm of J. Lauritzen set up a joint operation for the worldwide refrigerated cargo trade. This was designed to complement each of their own businesses by providing a fast, reliable and flexible service in the often seasonal variations of the trade. *Wild Curlew* and five others made it through from General Cargo Division to the Deep Sea Cargo Division era. All were sold by the middle of 1983. *Wild Curlew* had been built at Lubeck in 1973, her tonnages were 7,594grt and 9,169dwt, and she served until sold in 1981. The photograph shows a particularly smart looking vessel in earlier times displaying the Federal funnel marking. With four hatches and derricks, midships accommodation and a speed of 20kts, she was well suited for the trade. Yet, in due course even this business would transfer largely to the containerships, which could provide power sockets on deck for the 'ubiquitous boxes'. *Wild Cormorant* was an identical sister ship to this one.

104. STRATHDUNS →

As WW2 standard cargo ships faded out of service, Austin & Pickersgill launched their own replacement type of motor cargo ship. The first 'Standard Shelterdecker SD14' launched in December 1967, and the design with some variations, proved very popular worldwide with tramp and liner companies. Including licensee yards overseas some 203 of the approximately 15,000dwt ships, were built. Their rugged and reliable construction coupled with fuel and crew economy, plus a fair turn of speed led to a number of British liner companies ordering some. The original design had dimensions of 134.2m x 20.42m x 8.84m.dr, with 9,100grt. Depending on engine size fitted a fuel consumption of 22-25tpd could be realised, with speed in the range of 14-15.5 knots. Crew numbered 31, and the cargo gear in its most basic form consisted of 10 x 5ton derricks. In the photograph *Strathduns*, one of four remaining with P&O in 1981 is seen running light on draught, yet with an amazing collection of equipment as deck cargo. Other SD14s sold in 1981 were- *Strathdevon*, *Strathdirk* and *Strathdoon*, all having only entered service new between January 1975 and January 1977.

105.   WILD GANNET
Built at Drammen, Norway in 1977 this 9,592dwt fast refrigerated cargo ship operated for Lauritzen Peninsular Reefers' in their worldwide trade. She is seen in P&O colours in her latter days looking just a little 'sea-worn', yet pushing ahead with all the speed necessary for the job. Together with sister vessel *Wild Grebe*, she was sold during the Deep Sea Cargo Division period in 1983.

106. STRATHFIFE

On delivery from Mitsui, Japan in September 1978 this 17,350dwt vessel and sister ship *Strathfyne* would have been regarded as state of the art cargo ships. Decks and hatches were specially configured to allow the carriage of twenty and forty foot containers. A full set of crane-type derricks backed up a massive 300ton Stulcken heavy lift derrick for large indivisible cargo items. In April 1981 the ship was sold to OCL to handle residual general cargo traffic between the Gulf and the Far East as full containerisation spread. Both these ships continued to be managed by P&O, until OCL sold them in 1985. There is a fascinating footnote to relate here, since the two vessels just described were part of an order, subsequently cancelled in 1973, for a 400,000 ton VLCC! The order resurfaced in the form of two bulk carriers, again never built. In due course, apart from *Strathfife* and *Strathfyne*, three roll-on, roll-off cargo ferries were in the frame as part of the order value. *Ibex* and *Tipperary* did enter service, but the third failed to materialise!

107. STRATHETTRICK →

The final batch of cargo ships ordered by General Cargo Division had been the six Strath 'E's, from Poland's Gdansk Shipyard, for the UK/Gulf service. The class were of four hold, five hatch construction, with refrigerated cargo space available, to deliver between November 1977 and April 1979. Some eleven cranes were fitted plus a 300 ton Stulcken heavy lift derrick. *Strathettrick* illustrates well in the photograph just how far general cargo ship design had developed by the late 1970s. She is seen to be well laden with only a couple of containers and some heavy machinery on the deck and hatch tops. This ship went to OCL in 1981 with Management continuing until 1983. An interesting feature of this class and that of the Strath 'F's, was the integral design of the bridge front goal post mast structure. The topping lift for the derrick runs from the lower cross member of the radar and navigation light platform. Sister vessels were - *Stratheden*, *Strathewe*, *Strathelgin*, *Stratherrol* and *Strathesk*.

108.   BELLE ISLE

A link had existed between the British India Company and the Indian Ocean based Mauritius Steam Navigation Company. In the photograph, the 1971 built SD14, *Belle Isle* shows another variation in the outfitting of cargo gear. She was finally managed by P&O Deep Sea Cargo Division until sold in February 1984. Tonnages were 9,327 grt and 15,139dwt. See No.104 for technical details of the type. Sister vessel *Belle Rose* was sold in November 1983.

109.   KUBBAR

Danah, *Kubbar* and *Qarouh* belonged to a subsidiary of the Kuwait Shipping Co; and had been built by Hyundai, South Korea in 1978, as part of a class of very large cargo ships. Of 15,397grt and 23,618dwt, they were managed by Deep Sea Cargo Division in the 1981-1983 period.

SECTION 5.

The re-appearance of P&O Bulk Shipping Ltd; P&O Bulk Carriers Ltd, and the inception of P&O Ship Management Ltd, in 1984.

There had been management arrangements in place over the years covering other owners' ships, but in 1984 a new specialist entity arrived in the form of P&O Ship Management Ltd. This would in part absorb a not inconsiderable number of sea staff and shore staff into manning and operating outside vessels to the benefit of all. The service would be tailor made to the Owner's requirements, and might include the supply of officers, crew, storing, repairing, dry docking, technical backup and even, if so desired, commercial trading. Some of the vessels described in this section fall into this category. During the period involved dispersal of P&O's remaining cargo ships proceeded apace. Mention has been made under the individual gas ships of their sale in 1986 to Norwegian interests. However, ahead of this, in 1985 a 50% share of the newly formed P&O Gas Carriers Ltd, set up specifically to manage and trade the gas ship fleet, had been sold to the American company Overseas Shipholding Group – OSG. The fleet was made up of pairs of ships, so a split of the ownership of the ships between P&O and OSG was easily arranged, with the "odd" one, *Gambhira*, being jointly owned by both companies. A summary of such changes may be found in Appendix 2. At the end of 1982 and with full effect from January 1983, a major ship management contract involving the Abu Dhabi National Tanker Company's fleet of existing crude oil tankers, plus a new building programme, commenced. The contract was renewed until the end of 1990, when full technical control of the fleet joined their trading department in Abu Dhabi by Spring 1991. Also described below are a couple of exceptions to the normal scheme of things.

110.   SS BRITISH TRIDENT   and   111. SS BRITISH NORNESS

These two VLCCs were built by Mitsubishi, Japan in 1974 for demise charter to BP. Of 133,035grt and 261,011dwt *British Trident's* owner was Airlease International. The second ship, *British Norness*, had associations with Anglo Nordic and belonged to Norcape Shipping. This vessel's statistics were 132,942grt and 269,349dwt. Both ships bore a close resemblance to BP's 'R' class steam turbine powered VLCCs. The *British Trident* had a spell in lay-up in Brunei Bay from May 1983 to July 1986 when she resumed trading. Both ships re-delivered from BP to P&O in 1988 and were then sold onwards, with hand-over to new owners at dry docking.

112. MUNDOGAS PACIFIC

The history of this firm went back to 1956 and when P&O took a part interest in 1970 the Mundogas fleet consisted of eight gas tankers. The other parties involved at that time were Oivind Lorentzen of Norway, and Panaversal of Panama. The ship in this photograph was built in 1969 as *Fernwood*, one of three similar French built 16,500grt, 22,246m³ capacity gas carriers. *Fernwind* would later become *Mundogas Europe*, whilst the third of the series, *Fernvalley*, would also come under P&O Bulk Shipping Management, not from Mundogas, but from the Discaria Shipping Corporation's ownership as *Discaria*. *Mundogas Europe* and *Mundogas Pacific* went to other managers in 1981. *Discaria* remained with P&O Ship Management until 1985. The P&O interest in Mundogas was sold in 1984.

113. A28, YAMILAH at St.Nazaire →

The next four photographs are included to illustrate changes in tanker design and shipyard building techniques. At the very end of 1982 P&O Ship Management Ltd gained the contract to manage the three existing large crude oil carriers of the Abu Dhabi National Tanker Company. These ships would be joined at intervals during 1983, by the entry into service of seven new building product tankers of three specific classes. The new ships were to be overseen during the construction phase by P&O technical staff at shipyards in France and South Korea. The first new tanker, Yard No.A28 is seen in the latter stages of fitting out at the Chantiers de L 'Atlantique yard in St.Nazaire, France. A large hydraulic powered hose handling crane has replaced the traditional derricks. The ships building here, A, B, & C 28 were designed to comply with the very latest International Regulations for the construction of oil tankers, and this included provision of segregated ballast tank systems, (SBT). Designed for the carriage of four grades of clean petroleum product, the cargo pumps fitted consisted of 4 x 800m³/hr electrically driven centrifugal units. A B&W type main engine provided power to a controllable pitch propeller, and a shaft generator could supply the ship's electrical load once away on passage. An oil fired boiler and an exhaust gas boiler were fitted, plus an inert gas generator for cargo operations, etc. Sister ships in this class were B28, *Al Dhabiyyah*, and C28, *Arzanah* all of 27,900dwt. The two classes built in South Korea were of similar layout, but larger - two of 38,600dwt named *Umm Al Lulu*, and *Diyyinah*, with two of 57,200dwt named *Baynunah*, and finally, *Al Dhibyaniyyah*. The earlier three crude oil ships consisted of *Al Ain* 135,900dwt, *Al Dhafrah* 273,504dwt, and *Dalma* 265,120dwt. The fleet was operated and traded from the Owner's Abu Dhabi office, but technically managed from London until the end of 1990. The whole operation went 'in-house' in Abu Dhabi by April 1991.

114.   B28, AL DHABIYYAH

Still in primer, the accommodation block is nearing completion on the 27,945dwt vessel at St.Nazaire. The crane visible between accommodation and funnel was a dock side fixture.

115.   C28, ARZANAH, early construction.

This image clearly shows just how far modern ship building techniques have evolved to keep pace with demand, and remain competitive. This yard has been constantly modernised, and today builds many types of large ocean going vessel, including very large luxury cruise ships. The vast, tracked gantry crane can lift enormous sections of pre-constructed ship weighing hundreds of tons into place for welding, whenever ready. The dark grey block in the photograph is C28's accommodation block, awaiting construction of the hull for due attachment.

116.   ARZANAH

The profile of a product tanker built in the 1980s differed substantially to that of the 1960s. Crew numbers have nearly halved by way of much onboard automation, engines have become much more fuel efficient, whilst satellite communication and navigation systems are now standard kit.

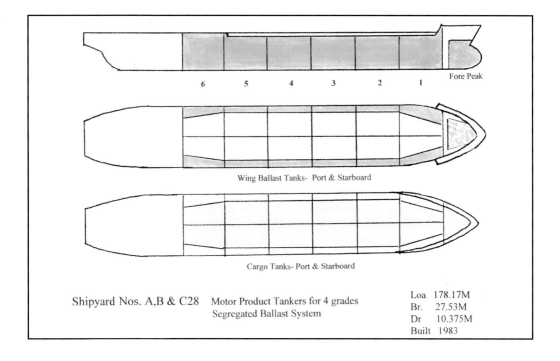

| | | | | | | Fore Peak |

6   5   4   3   2   1

Wing Ballast Tanks- Port & Starboard

Cargo Tanks- Port & Starboard

Shipyard Nos. A,B & C28   Motor Product Tankers for 4 grades
Segregated Ballast System

Loa   178.17M
Br.   27.53M
Dr   10.375M
Built 1983

SECTION 6.   The continuing Bulk Carrier Operation

Apart from one new bulker in 1986 the Company had come to rely more upon large 'chartered-in' ships to fulfil the various contracts of affreightment with raw material (iron ore and coal) producers and importers. This had formed the basis of the bulk carrier operation from the inception of Associated Bulk Carriers. However, a new form of charter was conceived by which ships were time chartered, but with an option to buy at certain set times over the duration of the charter. By this means, what had now become P&O Bulk Carriers Ltd, based in London, was able to maintain its presence in the bulk carrier trades. Later on, by exercising the purchase options at favourable prices, some of the time chartered ships came into P&O's beneficial ownership. In 1990 two new Korean built bulk carriers entered service under P&O ownership, and something of a resurgence began in the market, largely due to industrial expansion in the Far East. The ever increasing demand in that area for coal, oil and iron ore ensured more prosperous times for many shipowners, and yet the competition from Far Eastern owned fleets would be stronger than ever. Two more bulk carriers, the second *Duhallow* and *Eridge*, thus maintaining the historical naming of the bulk fleet ships, entered service in 1993. In 1994 and 1995, purchase options were exercised on two further previously chartered vessels – *Waterford* and *York* - and by 1997 the P&O Bulk fleet operationally stood at some eighteen large bulkers, with active involvement in any other ship type having long terminated. The year 1998 saw a major joint venture come to fruition with the Chinese industrial giant Shougang, who operated their own fleet of major bulk carriers. The blended fleet of some twenty six very large bulk carriers would be rebranded under a revival of the Associated Bulk Carriers' banner, with the Shougang vessels taking ABC traditional 'hunt' names. The entire operation was brought under P&O control early in 2000, and although the Company had looked at floating Associated Bulk Carriers possibly on the Norwegian Stock Exchange, ultimately a 50% interest was sold to Eurotower Holdings SA at the end of that year. At the same time, the operation and management of the fleet passed to London based Zodiac Maritime Agencies. Although direct involvement with the ships ceased in 2001, financial holdings in ABC continued to be reduced by individual ship sales until the exit strategy was finalised in December 2003. So ended P&O's almost half a century foray into all forms of bulk shipping and another chapter in the Group's long and illustrious history was brought to a close.

117. ORMOND

The photograph is seen courtesy of ©P&O Heritage Collection (DP World).

This ship delivered from Mitsubishi, Japan in March 1986 and at that time she was regarded as a large bulker indeed. Of 96,659grt, 187,025dwt *Ormond* not only became the fleet's largest, she was also the first commitment to new owned tonnage for a while. Dimensions were 300m. x 47.25m x 17.71m.dr, and her power plant consisted of a 6cyl. Mitsubishi-Sulzer developing 18,400bhp. Nine large side sliding hatch covers would become the norm amongst the world's largest bulkers as both loading and discharge ports became geared for this arrangement, at their respective deep water terminals. *Ormond* remained within the Associated Bulk Carriers fleet well beyond the year 2000, and is still in service today (2008).

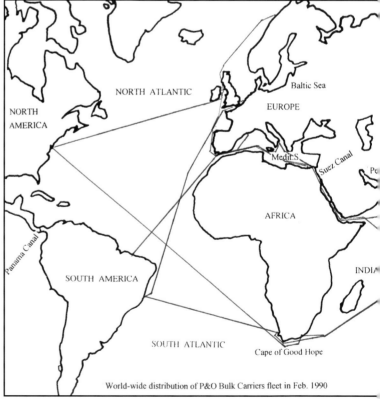

World-wide distribution of P&O Bulk Carriers fleet in Feb. 1990

118.   ZETLAND

Although this ship pre-dates No.117, she became time chartered to P&O Bulk Carriers in 1989. Built in 1985 by Hyundai, South Korea her original name had been *Mosbulk*. The ship's statistics were 74,003grt, 145,905dwt on dimensions of 877ft. x 141ft. x 57.3 ft. dr. In 1998 she was purchased by ABC and for the first time ever, since its adoption in 1965 for bulk ship names, the A to Z 'Hunt' naming system reached the end of the alphabet. Not unreasonably there was no ship name beginning with an 'X', although '*Exmoor*' was suggested.

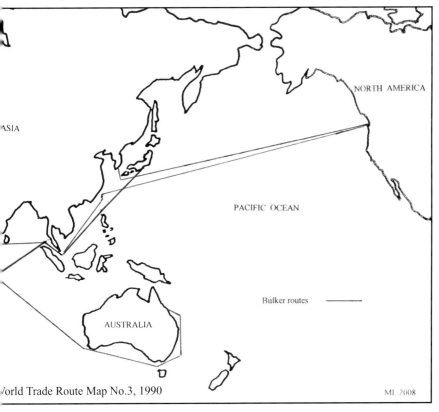

World Trade Route Map No.3, 1990

ML 2008

119. VINE

In 1990 P&O Bulk Shipping took delivery of a pair of new bulkers from Daewoo, South Korea in the form of this ship and sister vessel *Ullswater*. At 63,106grt and 114,976dwt, the dimensions were 266m. x 40.5m. x 14.52m.dr. with the standard nine hatch arrangement. A 13,770bhp KHIC B&W 5S70MC main engine provided a service speed of 14kts on about 47.7tpd of fuel oil. The ships were fitted with 2 x 2,000m³/hr electric centrifugal ballast pumps. The anchors each weighed 13,500Kg and the complement totalled 31 persons including four travel work squad. Both ships remained with ABC until the end. The fuel consumption makes an interesting comparison with that of the little steam tanker *Erne* of 1962 – she transported a cargo tonnage of about five and a half times less than *Vine*, yet required 5tpd more fuel in the process! In general this size group of bulkers had evolved in order to load a maximum cargo at Hampton Roads, Virginia, USA where a number of coal exporting facilities exist. Although vessels up to around 150,000 tons capacity could part load, water depths in the channels precluded deeper loading. After further deepening work in the 1980s the optimum size cargo lift reached approximately 110,000 tons. The ships in that category became known as 'baby capers' – to distinguish them from their larger 'round South Africa size' sisters.

120. BUCCLEUCH (2) →

Tell-tale coal dust on the hatch covers again gives the game away. Although of very impressive statistics, 90,820grt and 182,675dwt, this ship has the typical minimalist appearance of modern ships. The main deck above hatch top level is totally without features – not even small floodlight towers have been provided. An 'ABC' style emblem has replaced the P&O flag on the 1993 built ship's bridge front. Delivered by Tsuneishi Shipbuilding Company, Hashima, Japan in the September, her 18,750bhp main engine and single propeller could give a speed of 13.5kts at 73rpm. Some 201,247m³ of cargo stowage space was available. The crew totalled twenty six persons. The ship was transferred to Associated Bulk Carriers in July 1998 and passed to Zodiac Maritime Agency Ltd management in January 2001.

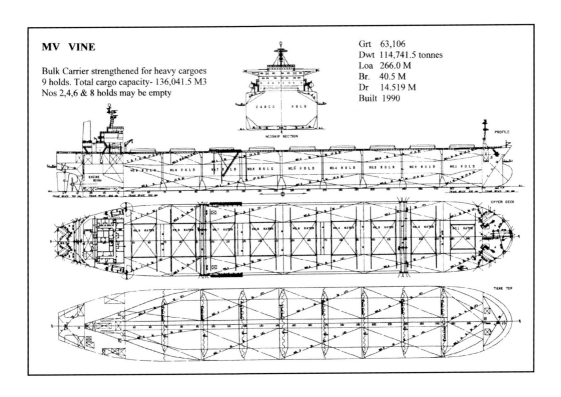

MV VINE

Bulk Carrier strengthened for heavy cargoes
9 holds. Total cargo capacity- 136,041.5 M3
Nos 2,4,6 & 8 holds may be empty

Grt   63,106
Dwt 114,741.5 tonnes
Loa   266.0 M
Br.   40.5 M
Dr   14.519 M
Built 1990

121. KILDARE (2)

Most of the early bulk names were reused on second generation bulk ships, and the vessel makes an interesting comparison to the previous holder, the 'OBO' of 1972. At 211,320dwt this large bulker could easily stow an extra 50,000 tons of cargo. The 1996 version had been built for Shougang as *SGC Express*. Dimensions were 312m x 50m. x 18.32m.dr. The final 'ABC' dark blue funnel and motif can just be seen in this view off Dungeness Point.

122. MEYNELL (2)

Built in 1997 as *SG Universe*, the second ship of the name measured 93,629grt and 185,767dwt on dimensions of 292m x 48m x 18.02m.dr. A B&W 7cyl. Engine produced 21,650bhp for a speed of 13.75kts.

BIBLIOGRAPHY

E.C.Talbot-Booth	Merchant Ships 1949-1950	------
R.Carpenter	Modern Ships	1970
Laurence Dunn	British Passenger Liners	1959
Laurence Dunn	The World's Tankers	1956
David Howarth & Stephen Howarth	The Story of P&O	1986

ACKNOWLEDGEMENTS

I would like to record my thanks and appreciation to all the kind individuals who with their time, information and material, have so helped with the compilation of this book, in particular, John Alcock, Christine Bentley, Susie Cox, Beth Ellis, Stephen Lewis, Doreen Miller, Phil Neumann and Stephen Rabson.

PHOTOGRAPHIC SOURCES

© P&O Heritage Collection (DP World) - 4,73,95,100,117

© Fotoflite - 3, 5, 6, 8, 9, 24, 30, 51, 55, 56, 59, 63, 64, 65, 74, 78, 79, 80, 81, 82, 83, 86, 87, 93, 94, 96, 97, 98, 99,101,102,103,104,105,106,107,108, 109, 110, 111, 112, 118, 119, 120, 121, 122.

APPENDICES

1. Vessels not included elsewhere in illustrations or text
2. Company Timetable of Events.
3. Origin of ships' names.
4. Head Office locations in London
5. Associated Bulk Carriers Fleet List 1998

APPENDIX 1

Vessels not included elsewhere in illustrations or text

Tankers-
NORDIC SPIRIT   b.1978   81,131dwt ex Anglo Nordic vessel
        Renamed- EASTERN ENTERPRISE 1981
             "   RUTLAND (1)   3/1987
             "   CONSTITUTION   6/1988 when sold to Conoco.

ENERGOS *   b.1975   18,939grt, 31,102dwt ex MOBIL REFINER   11/10/91-1/09/93
LUMIERE   b.1972   14,167grt, 24,957dwt.   11/10/91-22/06/93
Both vessels ex Cunard's, * H.E.Moss & Co's product tankers.
* Only managed by H.E Moss & Co.
Dates shown are for P&O management only.

Gas Tanker-
NEWMARKET   b.1977   982grt,1.125dwt, 1,504m³ ex KYOSEKI MARU
Managed in 1987 for Cheltenham Holdings, Panama.

OBOs-
RANGER   b.1972   51,402grt,101.700dwt.
ROVER   b.1973   52,699grt,101,800dwt
Initially chartered as 'dry bulkers' but converted back to 'OBO' status by P&O in 1985. Managed for Panther Shipping. RANGER sold 1988, ROVER sold 12/87.

Bulkers-
PYTCHLEY (1)   b.1980 109,488dwt   ex NORTHERN GALE   (1986-1997)
QUORN (1)   b. 1983 63,800dwt   ex MALVERN   (11/86-1988)
SNOWDON (1)   b.1983 131,650dwt   ex CETRA SAGITTA   (1987-1991)

Reefers- ex Deep Sea Cargo Division
WILD FLAMINGO   b.1973 6,925grt   sold 1983
WILD FULMAR   b.1974 6,925grt   "
WILD MALLARD   b.1968 9,504grt   ex MATAURA '8/77   sold 1981
WILD MARLIN   b.1968 9,504grt   ex MANAPOURI '11/77   sold 1982

Containership-
STRATHCONON b.1978   15,762grt, 21,178dwt (GCD,1980. sold OCL 1982)

APPENDIX 2

Company Timetable of Events

1955 The original P&O Group plan envisaged a fleet of tankers with a deadweight totalling some 500,000 tons capacity, all to be built in United Kingdom yards. The programme amounted to some twenty five vessels in two size categories-

18-19,000 ton clean product carriers and 36-37,000 ton crude oil ships. Delays in securing shipyard space and other factors led to alterations in ship sizes and numbers completed. The first vessel entered service in December 1958, and the total tonnage would duly be delivered and find good charters with the major oil companies.

1959-1962 The fourteen ships went into service under existing Group companies' ownership and management including the new Charter Shipping Company.

1962 Trident Tankers Ltd, was formed at the end of 1962 to manage and operate all of the Group's tankers collectively.

1964 P&O and Anglo Norness established the joint Bermuda operation Associated Bulk Carriers, to market a fleet of Bulkers, OBOs, O/Os. There were twenty seven vessels involved, with contracts of affreightment for such dry bulk commodities as coal and iron ore.

1965 The first of P&O's own dry bulk carriers came into service, and was placed under the control of a merged Hain-Nourse operation, although marketed by ABC.

In this year Overseas Containers Ltd, (OCL) arrived on the scene as the result of an agreement between P&O, British & Commonwealth, Furness Withy and Ocean Steamship Company. The objective being to develop and expand the containerisation of many existing specific general cargo trades, worldwide.

1966 The first of P&O's OBOs was placed under Trident control – they would be categorised as tankers when trading as such.

1967 As had happened briefly in 1956/7 the Suez Canal closed – this time due to the Middle East War. It would not fully re-open until 1975, leading to major disruption for cargo liner and tanker trades to and from the Middle and Far East. All traffic had of necessity to voyage around the whole of Africa, typically adding some 5,000 miles plus each way.

1969 P&O and Ocean Transport established the separate entity Panocean, to enter and participate actively in the growing worldwide chemical tanker trade.

1970 Trident had by now the largest fleet of independently owned oil tankers in the United Kingdom, outside of the major oil companies. With recent acceptance into the fleet of four 200,000 ton crude oil carriers, some twenty ships were in service this year. Four early steam tankers had been sold, seven new brought in, along with the first three motor OBOs.

1970 P&O acquired a part interest in Mundogas.

1971 New Group divisions were established as trade patterns altered and economies of operation sought:-

P&O General Cargo Division combined all of the Group companies' ocean cargo ships into one fleet.
P&O Bulk Shipping Division saw the merger of Trident Tankers Ltd with the bulk carrier fleet of Hain-Nourse Ltd. This new division would come to have a number of additional responsibilities relating to various partnerships and part owned entities, such as:- Associated Bulk Carriers, Panocean, Bulk Shipping Associates and LNG Carriers Ltd, the latter being a venture between P&O, A.P.Moller and Fearnley & Eger.

1971 P&O's Federal Steam Navigation and the Danish firm of J.Lauritzen set up Lauritzen Peninsular Reefers to operate fast refrigerated cargo services, worldwide. The 'Wild Reefer' ships went into action.

1972 The first gas tanker (LPG) entered service – (ordered in the Trident era).

1973 P&O acquired 50% interest in ABC partners Zapata Naess and the whole was renamed Anglo Nordic Shipping. That fleet stood at twenty five bulkers, OBOs, O/Os and tankers.

1975 The remaining ships in the General Cargo Division were renamed, and then operated under the 'P&O Strath Services Ltd' banner.

1976 Panocean's deep sea operation merged with Tate & Lyle's 'Anco' services to become Panocean-Anco. However , the coastal fleet remained a 50:50 P&O: Ocean company.

1978 Fearnley & Eger withdrew from LNG Carriers and the ship was duly renamed.

John Swire and Sons joined the Panocean-Anco partnership.

1980 Three GCD ships were transferred to OCL to handle residual Gulf-Far East general cargo traffic in the face of rapid containerisation of the trade.

Further changes to the Panocean-Anco partnership see Tate & Lyle depart and two new members join.

1981 In March, P&O Bulk Shipping Division and P&O General Cargo Division merged to form P&O Deep Sea Cargo Division, and further rationalisation of resources ensued.

1982 The last surviving vessel of British India's once four ship passenger/cargo Bombay-Gulf service was retired and sold.

Anglo Nordic was wound up, and control of ABC passed to P&O Bulk Carriers Ltd.

At the end of the year, a major ship management contract was gained involving the Abu Dhabi National Tanker Company fleet – ADNATCO. Three existing crude oil carriers were later joined during 1983 by seven new building product tankers from yards in France and South Korea.

1983 Panocean-Anco's deep sea ships went to a 'pool' operation with Stolt Nielsen. P&O and Ocean each now own three of the six ships they formerly owned on a 50:50 basis.

1984 Along with P&O Bulk Carriers Ltd, the title P&O Bulk Shipping Ltd now re-appears, plus the newly established entity P&O Ship Management Ltd.

P&O's interest in Mundogas is sold, as are its three Panocean deep-sea ships.

1985 50% of the P&O gas fleet (4 ships) was sold to the Overseas Ship Holding Group, of New York. The resulting operating company became known as P&O Gas Carriers Ltd.

1986 The entire LPG operation passed to the Norwegian Kvaerner Group Company, Mhyre Havtor, although some management of ships continued until 1987. With the subsequent sale of the single LNG carrier, P&O's gas tanker venture ended.

P&O acquired 100% of OCL and relinquished its 50% of the Panocean coastal operation to Ocean Transport, thus ending P&O's involvement with Panocean. P&O would rename OCL in 1987, when it became P&OCL.

1988 Two VLCCs, demise chartered to BP, re-delivered to P&O and were sold on.

1990 P&O acquired 50% of C.Rowbotham Ltd's coastal tanker fleet. This large fleet would see some involvement with new buildings in the Far East, but the firm kept its own operational and management structure, with technical support.

1991 Cunard's one remaining product tanker was brought into P&O, along with the company H.E. Moss & Co.

Ltd plus a single managed tanker, when P&O Containers Ltd acquired the cargo interests of Cunard-Ellerman.

Management of the Abu Dhabi National Tanker Company fleet passed fully to the Owner's Head Office in Abu Dhabi, between January and 30th April 1991.

1993 The remaining 50% share in C. Rowbotham Ltd was acquired and the company renamed P&O Tankships Ltd.

1996 In December, P&O Tankships Ltd, was sold to James Fisher of Barrow.

1998 P&O announced a forthcoming major joint venture in bulk shipping with the large Chinese industrial group, Shougang. The merged and expanded fleet would trade under a revived Associated Bulk Carrier (ABC) banner.

2000 Early in the year P&O acquired the Chinese half of ABC. At the end of the year 50% of the ABC holdings were sold to Eurotower Holdings SA, and the day to day operation and management of the fleet passed to Zodiac Maritime Agencies. The final 50% interest in ABC was sold to Eurotower at the end of 2003, thereby ending a P&O involvement in bulk shipping lasting nearly half a century.

APPENDIX 3

Origin of ships' names

The majority of names carried by both oil and gas tankers operated by Trident and P&O Bulk Shipping had been used before, Most stem from British India's and P&O's earlier years of trading to the Indian sub-continent area. Villages, towns, districts and state names have all found their way around the World, often on successive ships during the last century, or so. One later variant was the use of Scottish 'Ard' names for two classes of oil tanker. The following list is just a selection-

BUSIRIS	previously a J.& P. Hutchison steam coaster of 1929.
ELLORA	a British India cargo steamer of 1911.
ELLENGA	" "
FOYLE	used on a Hain tramp steamer of 1915.
GAMBADA	British India cargo steamers built between 1918-1920.
GAMBHIRA	" " " (second b.1939)
GANDARA	" " " (WW2 loss)
GARBETA	" " "
GARMULA	" " " (WW2 loss)
GAZANA	" " "
KENT	a Federal refrigerated cargo steamer of 1918
MALOJA	a P&O steam passenger liner of 1923 – 1st Company ship over 20,000t.
MALWA &	
MANTUA	two of a class of ten, P&O passenger/ cargo liners built 1903-1912.
QUEDA	British India cargo steamer of 1924
QUILOA	" " 1925 (WW2 loss)
TALAMBA	" " 1924 (Hospital ship in WW2)

One unique method of nomemclature resulted from the personal interest of the P&O Group chairman, Sir Donald Anderson, in 1965. A keen huntsman, he wisely reasoned that by utilising 'Hunt' names, there would be an alphabet long choice for this new class of vessel. The OBOs and one O/O carrier were brought into the system, and with the inevitable lack of an 'X', even a second generation of larger bulk carriers in the 1990s, would continue the theme. See page 48 table.

APPENDIX 4

Head Office locations in London

Trident Tankers began with just two rooms in No.122 Leadenhall Street in 1962.
A move to One Aldgate came in 1963.

The next move in 1965 was to the rather quaint 3, Bevis Marks to be followed by the third and fourth floors on return to One Aldgate.

In the 1970s a degree of Group consolidation saw Bulk Shipping Division and General Cargo Division occupy with others, the rambling edifice known as Commerce and Industry / Beaufort House along Middlesex Street, and not far from Aldgate underground station. In January 1985, P&O Bulk Carriers, Gas Carriers and Ship Management, made their final move to the top floors of the LWT Building at Upper Ground, Waterloo.

APPENDIX 5

Associated Bulk Carriers Fleet List August 1998

Vessel	Year	Flag		Summer Deadweight M/T
Jedforest	1997	Bahamas	Ex SG ENTERPRISE	211,485
Kildare	1996	Liberian	Ex SGC EXPRESS	211,320
Lauderdale	1997	Bahamas	Ex SG PROSPERITY	211,201
Ormond	1986	Bermuda		187,025
Taunton	1986	Bermuda	Ex MARINE CRUSADER	186,324
Meynell	1997	Liberian	Ex SG UNIVERSE	185,767
Newforest	1996	Liberian	Ex SGC FOUNDATION	185,688
Buccleuch	1993	Liberian		182,675
Pytchley	1996	Liberian	Ex SGC CAPITAL	179,869
Quorn	1996	Liberian	Ex SG CHINA	179,869
Snowdon	1998	Liberian		170,000
Rutland	1997	Liberian	Ex SG FORTUNE	170,013
Heythrop	1996	Panamanian		165,729
Irfon	1996	Panamanian		165,628
Cotswold	1986	Bermuda	Ex CHINA FORTUNE	151,016
Nord-Energy	1991	Danish		150,149
Aberous	1992	Panamanian		149,532
Waterford	1990	Bermuda		149,513
York	1990	Bermuda		149,503
Zetland	1985	Bermuda	Ex MOSBULK	145,905
Vine	1990	Bermuda		114,976
Ullswater	1990	Bermuda		114,741
Eridge	1993	Bermuda		114,031
Duhallow	1993	Bermuda		114,013
Grafton	1996	Bermuda		113,541
Fernie	1996	Bermuda		113,532

INDEX

Middleton Press

Easebourne Lane, Midhurst, West Sussex.
GU29 9AZ   Tel:01730 813169

EVOLVING THE ULTIMATE RAIL ENCYCLOPEDIA

www.middletonpress.co.uk   email:info@middletonpress.co.uk
A-978 0 906520 B- 978 1 873793 C- 978 1 901706 D-978 1 904474 E- 978 1 906008

OOP Out of print at time of printing - Please check availability   BROCHURE AVAILABLE SHOWING NEW TITLES